The Killing of Aarushi and the Murder of Justice

The Killing of Aarushi and the Murder of Justice

Rajesh Talwar

ISBN : 978-93-5324-261-9

First Published, 2020

Published by

Kalpaz Publications
C-30, Satyawati Nagar,
Delhi – 110052
Ph.: 011-47034999, 9811692060
www.kalpazpublications.com
E-mail: kalpaz@hotmail.com

Printed at: G. Print Process, Delhi

DEDICATION

For the innocents who suffer in wars not of their own making and those other innocents who suffer even in peacetime, and languish in prison cells for crimes that they did not commit

Talwar residence (Second floor)

L-32, Jalvayu Vihar, Sector 25, Noida

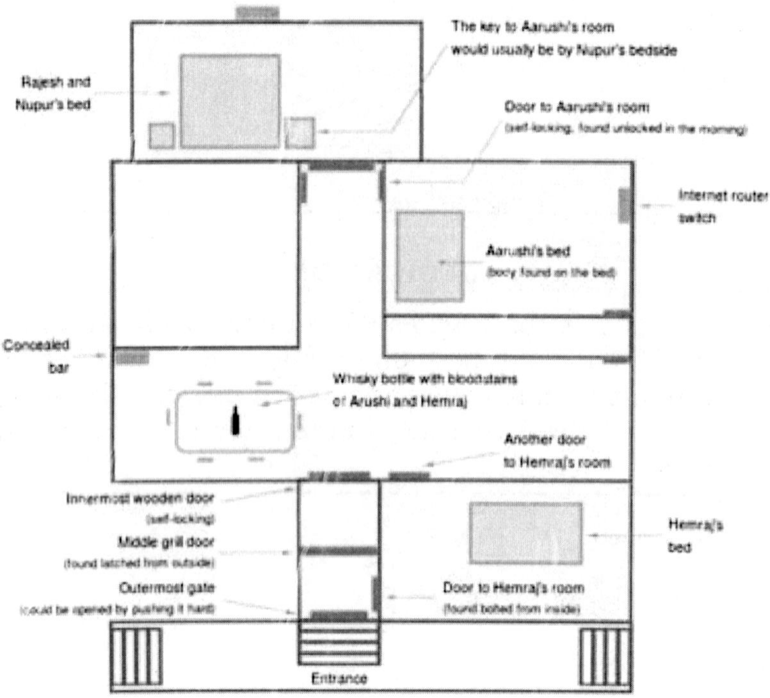

Source: Wikipedia

Note: It may be noted that the middle door detailed in the map is a mesh door, and the outermost door an iron grill door. The gap between the innermost door and the middle door is not to scale.

Contents

Synopsis

The Aarushi Talwar-Hemraj Banjade murder case gripped the imagination of the nation for the better part of a decade and is likely to remain a running story for many more years. The case involved the shocking and heinous murder of a young teenage girl, Aarushi and the family servant Hemraj, and was first investigated by the state police that allowed the crime scene to be heavily contaminated and robbed of all direct evidence. The case took many twists and turns, which were widely reported in the media. Initially the Talwars, Nupur and Rajesh, dentists and parents of the young girl were suspected of the crime by the state police, but subsequently when investigation was handed over to the Central Bureau of Investigation (CBI), the country's premier investigative agency, the first team investigating the matter reached the conclusion that the Talwars were innocent and it was Hemraj's associates that had committed the murders. The case took another turn when a fresh investigating team was put in charge following the appointment of a new director. This new team exonerated the servants and directed the needle of suspicion once more towards the Talwars. In the trial that followed the Talwars were found guilty and sentenced to life imprisonment.

Many questions, however, still remain. This book considers some of those unanswered questions, examines the judgement and related material closely in the context of three possible scenarios, and concludes that the Talwars were probably innocent and should at any rate been given the benefit of reasonable doubt. The author of two bestselling books on the Nirbhaya case and on the vanishing of Subhash Chandra Bose makes a compelling case as to why the Aarushi Talwar murder case remains one of the most debated, but ultimately unsolved, crimes of this century.

Disclaimer

This book is an attempt to provide rational analysis and accurate information with regard to the Aarushi Talwar and Hemraj Banjade murder case. However, it is written with the understanding that the author is not making any authoritative pronouncements on the matter, and that speculative logic, reasoned suggestions and hypothesis are well within the prerogative of an author's license on such a controversial and inconclusive matter, especially since the case is no longer active in the courts, and is pending the hearing of an appeal by the high court. Much of what follows in the book is necessarily speculative. The author had a choice to simply remain silent on the issue and await the eventual hearing of the appeal by the Allahabad High Court or venture to offer an unbiased analysis of the judgement in the greater public interest and good. In the process of theorising and imagining three possible scenarios that have been outlined in this book the author sincerely regrets any hurt or pain caused to any person(s). Furthermore, the author does not wish to impugn the integrity and competence of any member of the police, investigative agencies and the judges that deliberated on the vexed issues covered in this book beyond what was strictly necessary, in his view for a fair and unbiased analysis of the issues covered in this book. Finally, what follows represents the author's personal views and no other individual or organisation bears any responsibility for it.

Acknowledgments

I would like to express my special thanks to Professor Manjula Batra, Dean, Faculty of Law at the Jamia Millia Islamia for our discussions on subjects covered in the book. Among my work colleagues I would like to express thanks to Nasser Zakr, Kaoru Okizumi, Alhagi Marong, Joanna Paul, Nicholas Perez, Zubair Ahmad, Frozish, Samira, Gunmala Kala, Surya, Simon and Emma Hibling. A word of thanks for Kumkum Jain, who is always very generous with her archived material and her views.

Additionally, for their encouragement, advice and suggestions, I would like to thank Niharika, Tum Zinta, Kareesha, Yoon, Sanjay Kumar, Anita Misra, Virender Kumar Garg, Sanjiv Talwar, Sumit Talwar, Simi Talwar, Alka Talwar, Abhishek, Abhinav, Geetanjali Talwar-Shah, Puneet Shah, Praveen Kumar Talwar, Neha Talwar, Sakshi Talwar, Smita-'Pinky', Poonam, Shubha, Mitro, Bindu, Sanjay Rattan, Narendra Laljani, Karin, Narendra Singh, Shakun, Cheeku, Jacob Zachariah, Mini, Mitro, Nirmal Sharma, Pamela Sharma, Deepti Mehrotra, Pamela, Roopali, Nasser Zakr, Nasir Enam Khan, Chandra Mohan, Sagari Chabbra, Avi, Laxmi Kant, Vali, Rashmi J, Ramola and Sabita Sharma-Joshi. Finally, I would like to thank Sanjana Roy Choudhury who did a marvellous edit of the manuscript, paying great attention to detail. This book has been vastly improved as a result of her efforts.

Preface

The idea of writing a book on the Aarushi Talwar and Hemraj Banjade murder case had crossed my mind a couple of times over the years, but there were a few reasons why I decided against it. Firstly, because I live and work overseas, it isn't always possible to keep abreast of stories in India even in this age of the Internet. I would need to attend trial court hearings, meet with the accused couple and given the time constraints of my professional life this would simply have not been possible. Another reason is that the way the story was spun out in certain sections of the press – and we are all susceptible to media manipulation – I (together with most of those that followed the case) concluded that the middle-aged dentist couple was, in fact, guilty of the crime of murdering their teenage daughter, Aarushi and domestic help, Hemraj.

There was additionally one other factor. This had to do with justice or at any rate, my perception of it. I didn't doubt that the Talwars would get justice from the courts. They were not short of money; in fact they hired the best lawyers that money could buy. Even the relatively rich think twice before they go on to hire the likes of Harish Salve, senior advocate, a Nani Palkhiwala protege, who charges lakhs for a single appearance in the Supreme Court. The Talwars didn't seem to have a shortage of legal talent to represent them and their interests and made frequent forays to the Allahabad High Court and the Supreme Court.

In financial terms the Talwars were not underdogs. The assumption that I (and others) made was that it was the poor associates of their erstwhile servant Hemraj who needed to be protected from the relative money power of the Talwars who might get them trapped. After all, the Indian police don't have the cleanest image in the world. It was possible, the enlightened middle-class told itself, that the police had been paid off to get the guilty, but influential, Talwars off the hook and to pin the crime on some poor scapegoat. Those who considered themselves to be progressives did not wish to support the modern day distortion of the age-old biblical maxim of the sons paying for the sins of the fathers "let the servants take the rap for the employers. Some say this is replayed out in the case of a film star charged with mowing down people sleeping on the pavement with his SUV – but that is a discussion for another time.

So, what happened that changed my mind and made me realise that the Talwars were probably innocent victims of a crime played out in our courts every day? In October 2015, I was at the Delhi airport to catch a connecting flight to Bangkok. I had time on my hands, saw the book *Aarushi* by Avirook Sen selling at the airport bookstore and picked it up for my onward journey. I kept reading during much of the four and a half hour flight and continued reading through the night after I had checked into my hotel in the Prathunam area. My only misgiving in an otherwise brilliant book was how it sought to suggest in some fashion that the testimony of Hemraj's associates under the administration of a truth serum should have been given more weightage by the courts than it was. There were however many aspects about the case built up against the Talwars that were both shocking and deeply troubling.

On my way back to Kabul I broke journey in New Delhi to visit and stay with my parents in NOIDA. The film *Talvar* was running at the time to favourable reviews in the press. I decided to go and see it. Incidentally, a potential alternative title for the film was *NYODDA*, ultimately rejected by the producers, as it could have been offensive to the residents of the planned city adjoining the capital. The film carried a ring of authenticity, testimony to the hard work put in by the writers, actors and director. At the same time the film was strongly tilted in favour of the Talwars and against Hemraj's associates. This was both troubling and completely unnecessary. The film, like the book, was posing the question as to who was *more likely* to have committed the murders, a question that is completely irrelevant from a legal perspective. *Ethically speaking, the filmmakers should have done the 'who was more likely to have committed the murders' comparison only if they had clearly stated and emphasised that the case was never convincingly proved against anyone, neither the Talwars nor Hemraj's associates.* This was, however, not done. In my view, the focus of the film and the book should have been that the case was *not* proved beyond all reasonable doubt against either the Talwars or Hemraj's associates. The killer/s could have been someone else; someone who did not come under the radar of the investigators. We do not *have* to 'get' someone. Nonetheless, since it is the Talwars that are in prison, given the absence of evidence and proof sufficient for a conviction to be sustained, the shock I first experienced from reading the book increased after I watched the film.

That same evening I met up with an old friend and former colleague, Professor Manjula Batra, dean at the Faculty of Law, Jamia Millia Islamia. We discussed the movie at some length. Midway through the conversation, the idea of writing a book on the subject was brimming in my mind. What vestigial doubts remained, all but disappeared when I printed off a copy of Judge Shyam Lal's verdict and read it on the flight back to Afghanistan. I knew after reading the judgment that I needed to do something that would raise questions about the ignominies to which my namesake and his better half have been subjected to over the course of the past years – humiliation that continues to persist till this day, as even in jail they are sometimes brought out and paraded in the presence of VIP visitors like animals in a zoo.[1]

To reiterate, the point that both the film *Talvar* and book *Aarushi* miss is that it isn't who was more likely to have committed the murders; under the law of the land everyone is presumed innocent until proven guilty and no one can be convicted till the case against them has been proved beyond all reasonable doubt. And so despite the evident merit of the book and the film on some important aspects, I have very strong disagreement. In this book I offer up my own 'corrective,' grounded I hope, in facts and fair analysis if not in weighty, argument.

A few words about the title. This is a book about two killings or murders as the case may be; that of teenager Aarushi and Hemraj, the Talwar family's servant. In an ideal world the killing of any innocent person is not less important than that of another. Alas, we do not live in an ideal world, and so the focus of the title had naturally to be on the killing of Aarushi than on Hemraj, both because of her relative youth and because the latter's murder is generally thought of as being incidental or ancillary to the motive behind Aarushi's killing. Aside from these factors, there were practical considerations that prevailed against having a title such as *The Killing of Aarushi Talwar and Hemraj*. It would have been far too lengthy with the follow on clause *The Murder of Justice*, something I wished to retain.

At this juncture I would like to assert that in legal parlance the two terms " 'murder' and 'killing' are not interchangeable. Murder does not include an accidental killing. According to the prosecution Rajesh Talwar accidentally killed Aarushi; the blow that was meant for the servant landed on her head instead. In this book, however, I have not used these two words in a strict legal sense but often interchangeably and more as synonyms.

The title to Part One coincides with the prosecution's eventual conclusion and thrust, viz 'Dr Rajesh Talwar and Dr Nupur Talwar Murdered Aarushi and Hemraj'. It commences with an outline of the prosecution's case of who committed the murders, why they were carried out, and how they were executed. I discuss and critique both the judgement and the case for the prosecution, and try to explain why in my view the parents could *not* have been the killers.

The title to Part Two, i.e. 'The Servant's Associates Committed the Two Murders' is derived from the original CBI team's supposition in this case, which was that the Talwars were innocent and it was the deceased servant Hemraj's associates that committed the crimes. Those familiar with this case know the police investigation did two turnarounds. The state police investigators initially built up the case against the Talwars; the case was then handed over to the CBI, and the first investigating team headed by Deputy Inspector General Arun Kumar concluded that the Talwars were innocent and built up a case against the associates of Hemraj.

When this case against the servant's associates, Krishna and Rajkumar, was going to be presented to the court, to the Talwars' immense misfortune a new CBI director took over. A forensic report implicating the servants turned out to be erroneous and a mere typographical error. As a consequence there remained little, or no hard, evidence that could be presented against the two aforementioned. There was now a new investigating officer in charge, who then reverted to the original theory that the parents were guilty of the two murders. Part Two digs up the CBI's team one's theory of the servants' guilt and recreates a scenario where this was possible. Whereas the hypothesis that found the Talwars guilty was based on Rajesh Talwar finding his daughter in a sexually compromising position with the servant that sent him into a rage and killing spree, the alternative theory that held Hemraj's friends guilty, was built on the premise that Aarushi was sexually violated, or an attempt was made to sexually violate her. Be that as it may, following the assault on Aarushi, Krishna and Rajkumar killed her together with the servant Hemraj.

Part Two dwells on this scenario and details the pros and cons of this theory.

Part Three incorporates a work of fiction within its body, unusual for a book of this nature. Titled 'Someone Else Killed Aarushi and Hemraj', it may seem disjointed to some readers, but this is deliberate. *The Murder That Wasn't* is a short story to be read just like any other work of fiction. The story does not explain, by any means, all the peculiarities of the case. It does, however, challenge some of the assumptions made by the prosecution and accepted by the courts. It suggests, contrary to those assumptions that an outsider could have gained access to the apartment even without keys and further, that a single person could have carried a dead body to the terrace.

Part Four, the final part of this book is titled 'The Murder of Justice' somewhat dramatically, but justifiably, as I will endeavour to show. Using the Aarushi-Hemraj case as illustrative it takes a pan-India look at how justice in criminal matters is dispensed by the Indian courts.

In Dasna jail, Rajesh Talwar must have cursed himself innumerable times (as he might still be) for not having done some things differently. Simple, mundane stuff like getting a noisy air-conditioner fixed so that if you have a daughter sleeping in the next room who shouts for assistance (for whatever reason) you can hear her cries for help. This is, of course, yet more important if you have a daughter who happened to be suffering from laryngitis.[2]

Those who believe that it was the Nepali servant Hemraj's associates that sexually assaulted Aarushi that night will suggest a different lesson to be imbibed: Don't employ a male servant if you have a teenage daughter. Your trust in your servant may not be misplaced, but he will have male friends that may not be above suspicion.

Could Rajesh Talwar have done something differently that night that may have somehow saved his daughter? Telephone records accessed by the police show that

Aarushi's friend, Anmol had tried to reach her the same night first on her mobile and then on the landline around midnight, but his calls went unanswered, if not unnoticed. Had either Rajesh or Nupur answered the phone that night and called Aarushi to take the call, who knows things may have turned out differently. There can be fewer things more painful for a father than to realise he could do nothing to help his daughter at a time when she needed him most, when ironically enough he slept only a few feet away from her bed.

Some readers may pick up this book in the mistaken notion that the author is Dr Rajesh Talwar himself. They might still buy it on the assumption that I am perhaps a relative of the Talwars or privy to some special information. I wish to disabuse such a reader of this notion and assure him or her that this is not the case; I have never met the dentist or his wife.

There is, however, a connection, or rather a few things that my namesake and I share in common. We belong to a similar age group and both of us live, or lived, in NOIDA around the time the tragedy took place. And we both sport a half-beard and play table tennis for recreation.

In India, at airport immigration counters and hotel receptions I have sometimes been given a second look as if the person is confirming: 'Is this him?' They often have a questioning look and I gently shake my head. All this happened much more frequently earlier when the unfortunate event was fresh in everyone's mind and the Talwars were out on bail.

Although I have never met Dr Rajesh Talwar, I nearly did so barely two weeks before Aarushi's brutal killing. I was home for a two-week break. Sophisticated dental care was not available in the conflict zone I was stationed at, and a wisdom tooth giving me trouble. My mother brought up my namesake.

'Mrs Subramanium speaks highly of him. Seems to be very good,' she said.

'Isn't his wife also a dentist?'

My mother nodded, and added that the dentist couple's clinic was in Jal Vayu Vihar, a five-minute drive from our residence in Arun Vihar. Somehow that didn't work out and I eventually went elsewhere.

And then barely two weeks later it happened: the gruesome killings that the national media would follow as a running story for many years to come.

While the media, especially social media has sometimes played a positive role, for instance in getting the police to act in the Tarun Tejpal alleged rape case, on other occasions it has worked to the disadvantage of the innocent. This has been the case, I believe with the Talwars in the Aarushi-Hemraj murder case. In that context it is to be hoped that judges are less susceptible to manipulation by the media. It was therefore especially unfortunate to read a comment in the papers made by a high court judge to the effect that there was no need to hear the Talwars' appeal on an urgent basis – they did not have another child they could murder.

But that is another subject, for another book.

I have extensively reviewed the judgement during the course of writing this book. The judgement itself runs into 240 pages and at close to 60,000 words is the size of a full-length novel. The need for such a lengthy judgement is highly debatable, but before we start to criticise Judge Lal, we need to understand that he was merely emulating his betters; Supreme Court judgements often go on and on. Length is sometimes justified but often unnecessary. Mark Twain once famously quipped: 'I did not have time to write a short letter, so I wrote a long one instead.'

As we now know, Judge Shyam Lal had enlisted the support of his son, Ashutosh, also a lawyer, to help him choose the right words and fancy rhetoric and he had infact started to write the judgement *before* hearing the arguments for the defence. In defence of the judge one could argue that he was perhaps only setting out the outline of the judgement and the arguments raised by the defence have been duly incorporated in the judgment. On the other hand, those inclined not to give him the benefit of the doubt (since he refused to give the Talwars that very benefit) will argue that this only serves to demonstrate that the arguments for the defence were completely irrelevant. Saza Lal – as the judge was nicknamed by lawyers in the courts at Ghaziabad – had already made up his mind. He was only pretending to listen.

Great attention is paid by the judge to the opening paragraph of his judgement and his background in English Literature (in which he has a Masters) may have contributed to this, but as you continue reading you find that the grammar and syntax are less well maintained than one might expect from a senior judge with his background and the language too becomes progressively denser, unclear and often difficult to interpret.

Avirook Sen, the author of *Aarushi* is mystified at Judge Shyam Lal's references in his judgement to 'willy' and 'pecker' as substitute words for penis. During the course of an interview he even asks the judge if these are words he has perhaps come across in other judgements. Judge Lal knew, as every experienced draftsman and student of literature knows that for better reading, the same word should not be repeated too often. What Sen may possibly have not realised is that the judge probably sat down with a thesaurus and picked up synonyms without the understanding that his choice of words substituting the penis was not ideal, being more representative of vernacular slang which was hardly appropriate for formal, judicial language.

Moving from style to substance, in my view, the judgement is not only faulty; it amounts to a gross miscarriage of justice. Hence, the second part of the title to this book.

In writing this book I have principally relied on the text of Shyam Lal's judgement, court documents placed on the CBI website including its closure report, features, writings and books on the subject, and press reports and video material that is available in the public domain.

A short list of characters is included consisting mostly of the Talwars themselves, other possible suspects, investigating officers, doctors, and judge.

Finley Peter Dunne, the American humourist and writer famously remarked that 'an appeal... is when you ask one court to show its contempt for another court.' It is not the case that only judges can criticise the decisions of their brethren. No one should question that the courts ought to welcome criticism. Just recently, the Supreme Court of India hauled up General V.K. Singh, former chief of the armed forces for making certain unfortunate remarks in the context of a petition filed before the apex court related to his retirement age. The Supreme Court observed: 'We welcome criticism of our judgment but we don't welcome motives attributed to the court's judgment'.[3] Indeed, while the reader of this book will encounter extensive criticism of the Aarushi case judgement, including some black humour, there is no question of ascribing any ulterior motives to the judge himself whose judicial approach may have been misguided but honesty and integrity were above reproach.

On a related note the law of contempt of court has itself become antiquated in our country, as pointed out by Justice Markandey Katju.[4] Lord Atkin once observed: 'Justice is not a cloistered virtue. It must suffer the scrutiny and outspoken comments of ordinary men.'[5]

Lord Denning too made similar observations at greater length in his inimitable style.

'Let me say at once', he wrote, 'that we will never use this jurisdiction to uphold our own dignity. That must rest on surer foundations. Nor will we use it to suppress those who speak against us. We do not fear criticism, nor do we resent it. For, there is something far more important at stake. It is no less than freedom of speech itself. All that we ask is that those who criticize us should remember that from the nature of our duties, we cannot reply to their criticism. We cannot enter into public controversy. We must rely on our conduct itself to be its own vindication'.[6]

Every now and then so-called concerned citizens approach our courts in their private capacity and ask for warrants to be issued against such and such person on account of obscenity, offending religious sentiment, sedition, contempt of court, and what have you. A way must be found to keep such vigilantes in check, and preserve space so that people can freely express their opinions, even if they are unpalatable to some. Even if nothing comes out of such frivolous complaints they do succeed in dragging down innocent people to the courts and vitiating the air in which free and creative thought can flourish.

There may be some repetitiveness in the book. To some extent, this is both natural and inevitable, as the same set of facts need to be quoted with respect to different arguments that emerge. It is also partially deliberate as repetition can in some cases be an aid and not a nuisance, and I crave the reader's indulgence and patience.

One day I wish to have a meal with the Talwars when this is all over and they are set free. I hope for this to happen in the not too distant future, but cannot imagine how this will be possible given the infinitely slow churning wheels of Indian justice at all levels of the court system. But, about this failure of our criminal justice system, a bit later in the book.

RT

Kabul, Afghanistan;
30 March 2017

Part One

Dr Rajesh Talwar and Dr Nupur Talwar Murdered Aarushi and Hemraj

'Circumstantial evidence is a very tricky thing,' answered Holmes thoughtfully. 'It may serve to point very straight to one thing, but if you shift your own point of view a little, you may find it pointing in an equally uncompromising manner to something entirely different.'

– Arthur Conan Doyle

Presumed Innocent; Till Proved Guilty Beyond Reasonable Doubt

Before going any further, I would like to, for the benefit of the reader, mention three essential principles enshrined in the law with respect to criminal trials.

First and foremost, every accused person is presumed to be innocent, until his guilt is established beyond reasonable doubt.[7]

Secondly, not only does every criminal trial begin with this presumption, this presumption of innocence continues throughout the trial.[8]

Thirdly, the burden of proving the guilt of the accused falls on the prosecution, and unless it relieves itself of that burden the courts cannot record a finding of the guilt of the accused.[9]

The Case for the Prosecution

The testimony of A.G.L. Kaul, the investigating officer of CBI team two that prosecuted the Talwars for murder can conveniently double up as a summary of the case for the prosecution. His deposition, which was reproduced in *India Today,*[10] speaks of how sometime after midnight not long before the murders took place, Dr Rajesh Talwar heard a sound. He got up and went to the servant's room and found no one there...

Kaul goes on to testify as follows:

> *'There were two golf sticks lying in Hemraj's room, one of which Rajesh Talwar picked up. He heard a noise from the room of Aarushi.* ***The room was not locked and was just shut.*** *He opened the door and found Aarushi and Hemraj were in (an) objectionable position on the bed of Aarushi.'*

Only four lines into the narrative but already half a dozen inconsistencies are thrown up from the alleged facts and sequence of events. When Judge Shyam Lal wrote his judgement one of the arguments he presented against the involvement of an outsider in the attack was that Aarushi's room would have been locked. Here, the investigating officer's own version states that the room '*was not locked and was just shut*'. What about the auto-lock? It was obviously not operational as per the testimony, and we can therefore fairly assume that the door was not fully closed in team two's version of events. Kaul himself does not explain how and why the auto-lock had not clicked into place, and so the reader is forced to make an assumption that would create such a possibility.

So 'Baby Aarushi', to use an epithet used by Judge Shyam Lal for the teenage girl, was having a go with the servant without even bothering to secure the door. This seems incongruous.

There were two separate motivations that the prosecution needed to establish. The first was the motivation for the parents to kill their daughter and servant, but prior to that they needed to explain what possessed Aarushi to have consensual sex with an elderly servant? It is not as if Aarushi had no male friends her own age. Then why? Even if for the sake of argument one accepts the suggestion that her teenage hormones were acting up, why would she choose Hemraj of all people? The prosecution was at a loss to explain this too.

Right at the start, before the CBI took over the case a theory promoted by the state police was doing the rounds, which sought to explain through convoluted and bizarre logic that Aarushi was making love to the servant out of revenge for her parents' wife swapping orgies. One can easily imagine a wife or husband being unfaithful to teach an unfaithful spouse a lesson, but to extend that logic to a young teenage girl represents the mental churnings of a warped mind. Even if we give some credence to this perverse *and completely unsubstantiated theory*, which we should not, can we believe that not only Aarushi but Hemraj too, was brazen enough to go ahead and have sex without even bothering to lock the bedroom door?

> *'There were two golf sticks lying in Hemraj's room, one of which Rajesh Talwar picked up.'*

According to Kaul's testimony, Rajesh Talwar picked up a golf stick *before* he entered Aarushi's room. Why? Did he already suspect something? We do not know the answers to these questions. Rejecting this part of the prosecution's version the judge writes, a little more sensibly, in his judgement that Rajesh Talwar rushed to get the golf club *after* he discovered his daughter and the servant in a sexually compromising position.

In his cross examination Kaul then goes on to state that having found his daughter and the servant in an objectionable position Rajesh Talwar became so enraged that he immediately struck Hemraj's head with the golf stick. By the time he gave a second blow the servant's head moved from the position and the stick hit Aarushi on her forehead.

As further reported Kaul said the noise generated in the process awoke Nupur Talwar who rushed to Aarushi's room. Here the story turns yet more unbelievable.

'By the time the injured Hemraj had fallen from the bed,' Kaul states. 'Both checked the pulse of Aarushi and found her near-dead *which scared them* and *planned that the servant should be executed* so that no one comes to know about the incident.'

This then is the motivation for the killings. Aarushi was hit accidentally and went into a near-dead state. What is alleged to have happened subsequently does not fit the sudden rage scenario at all. According to the prosecution both parents were present at the scene at this stage. With Aarushi in the throes of death, would that rage not immediately subside and her parents wish to rush her to hospital? The prosecution, however, alleges Rajesh Talwar became fearful *for his own safety.* Instead of panicking for their daughter's safety the parents became concerned she would now inevitably die, and her killing would be pinned on them. The other inconsistency here is that even assuming Rajesh Talwar flew into a rage following the alleged attack and near fatal injury to Aarushi, his wife Nupur had already entered the room. As a woman, wife and a mother would she not have prevailed upon Rajesh to calm down and try and get things under control?

Unperturbed, Superintendent Kaul continues with the narration of the sequence of events. Rajesh and Nupur, he says, wrapped Hemraj's body in a bedsheet and dragged him to the terrace where they slit his throat, covering the body with a cooler panel.

Why did they not just kill him in the room, by hitting his head a few times more with the golf club? Why bother taking him in a still alive condition to the terrace? Was there not the possibility that he would regain consciousness and try and fight back? Or did they presume they would be able to overpower him? And why slice his throat creating such a bloody mess?

The other issue is, if as the closure report states that the blunt object, the so-called golf club, had already caused the deaths, why was it necessary to sever the arteries and create a bloody mess? For good measure, the prosecution would almost certainly argue, to make sure that the two were well and truly dead.

Question: Would two qualified and experienced doctors, one of them a gold medallist, not know when a person was dead? Why on earth did they need to sever the arteries? Would it not be far more likely for the less knowledgeable servants to have done this as they were less trained to read the pulse, test breathing, feel the heartbeat and examine other such indicators of a death?

The common argument was that the precise slit to the throat was proof enough it was the doctor-couple that did it. I believe the truth to be exactly the opposite. Only an amateur, one who wasn't sure that the person was really and truly dead, and wanted to make sure that the case beyond the shadow of any doubt, would bother with slitting of the throat, not seasoned, professional doctors.

The other great mismatch that exists is between the principal investigating officer's statement in court and what the judge concluded regarding the exact place where Hemraj's throat was slit. The investigating officer claims to be certain that Rajesh and Nupur dragged the body to the terrace 'where they slit his throat'. On the other hand Judge Lal writes: '*It is* ***also possible*** *that after bludgeoning Hemraj with golf stick* (sic) *he was carried in a bed sheet by both the accused to the terrace when he was in a state of concussion and thereafter on the terrace his throat was slit and body was dragged*'. In other words the judge is not certain where Hemraj's throat was slit – before being taken to the terrace or after. The law provides that all the links must be clear – this is an important gap in the sequence of events.

Kaul then goes on to say that after returning to the room 'they dressed up the crime scene by arranging the bed sheet and toys'. He does not, however, stop to explain what the purpose was in dressing up the crime scene. What benefit did the Talwars hope to derive from this? Would it not in fact look odd that someone other than themselves would have had the time at their disposal to dress up the crime scene? Why would they perform actions that could end up implicating them?

Finally, Kaul added that the Talwars slit Aarushi's throat to ensure that the wounds on Hemraj and their daughter looked similar and Nupur cleaned her private parts.

Kaul spoke about the scenario as if he was present there but of course he wasn't; there was no eyewitness or direct testimony in this case. The visual he paints is completely untrue to life. As I go on to argue in this section of the book, the circumstantial evidence all points to the innocence of the Talwars.

The Importance of the 'Near-dead' Theory

The motive is central to a crime. The following motive emerges from the testimony of the investigating officer.

> *'Both checked the pulse of Aarushi and found her near-dead which scared them and planned that the servant should be executed.*

The psychological implausibility of the scenario the investigating officer creates in the context of a sudden rage killing seems to be beyond his understanding.

It is theoretically possible that Dr Rajesh Talwar wounded both Aarushi and Hemraj with the golf clubs, went up to the terrace with Hemraj's injured body, severed his neck there, then went back down to Aarushi's room and did the same with his daughter. In terms of plausibility this is an extremely weak scenario that lacks the killed-in-an-uncontrollable-rage state of mind that was the entire foundation and basis for the prosecution's case against the Talwars.

While it is possible that Nupur Talwar would have assisted her husband in carrying Hemraj's already dead body upstairs, it is not at all credible that she would have carried his wounded body upstairs *with the intent to murder him on the terrace.* Carrying a full-grown man's body up the terrace is an exhausting process and in most cases will end any fit of rage that a person might have experienced. And certainly those strong emotions most likely would have passed by the time the couple came down to the apartment once again. To posit that this rage continued and Nupur permitted her husband to then sever her daughter's neck is possible but nevertheless an argument difficult to digest.

Water on the Bed sheet

Water was found on the bed sheet beneath Aarushi's body, which gave rise to the theory that the parents cleaned her private parts. Why would they do this? The prosecution argued that the Talwars didn't want anyone to know their daughter had been having sex, more so with the servant; they wished to protect their reputation. Who else, the argument continued, would have any motivation to clean her body parts?

The wet bed sheet beneath Aarushi's private parts does raise the suspicion that 'something' was cleaned, possibly her pyjamas, possibly her private parts, possibly both, but is it not likely that an assailant who had raped or attempted to rape her may have done this?

The pyjama was found dry, which does make for a logical inference that it was the pubic region that had been cleaned.

The theory that Hemraj's associates had murdered both Aarushi and him is discussed in the next segment of this book, but it is worth pointing out that Krishna and Rajkumar who were the prime suspects at one stage, also had a possible motivation to clean up Aarushi's pubic area if any one of them had in fact attempted to violate her. This presumes of course that they were thinking clearly and did not panic at the thought that their actions might wake up either of the parents.

With the onset of Internet, easy access to information and popularisation of crimes serials there is an increased awareness and it isn't impossible now for people to know that body fluids such as semen can be matched. It is likely that prior to her murder, Aarushi was sexually violated. No semen was found inside Aarushi's vagina, as per the post-mortem but as Judge Shyam Lal observes in his judgement this does not necessarily mean that she was not sexually violated. It is also possible that a would-be rapist lost control and ejaculated before penetration. If this was indeed the case, having been schooled in the possibility of identification through body fluids, after the killing the perpetrator may have immediately realised that he had to clean up the mess.

The Assumption that the Talwars were Stupid

Rajesh and Nupur Talwar were not stupid. They could not have simply assumed that the police would not go to the terrace. As a matter of fact the terrace was the most natural place for the investigators to search the murder weapon. At this point it was far from clear to the Ghaziabad police conducting the investigation how exactly Aarushi's killing had taken place. The terrace was the most logical place to search for a weapon or clues. A lock would have been no barrier for an investigating team. Moreover a dead body would have started to give out a stench sooner than later. Surely, at the time, Rajesh Talwar did not have foreknowledge, prescience or so little faith in the investigative abilities of the state police that he imagined that a lock would hold them off.

Why would Rajesh Talwar implicate Hemraj? The argument that he and Nupur thought that after the discovery of their daughter's killing they would still have the solitude and privacy in their flat to somehow carry Hemraj's dead body from the terrace to their car below and get rid of it in the Ganda Nala doesn't sound plausible. If they were indeed the killers the only real alternative was to continue to hammer Hemraj with whatever hard object was available, get his body into a sack, carry it to the car and get rid of it. An intelligent killer would have most likely worked in this way, and they would have done all this *before* Aarushi's death was announced; that was the way to do it and escape detection. The severing of an artery would also be an act of colossal stupidity, especially for qualified doctors. They would have known how difficult it would be to get rid of all the blood on the terrace.

To think that Rajesh and Nupur, on their return after immersing Aarushi's ashes in the Ganges at Haridwar would assume that Hemraj's body would not start rotting and inevitably come to the notice of the neighbours if not the police, tests credulity. And that then they would somehow manage to get rid of the decaying and stinking corpse " carrying it down the staircase the same way they had allegedly taken it upstairs doesn't somehow wash. Did the investigating team believe that the couple was stupid enough to imagine it would be that easy to get rid of the body in a crowded township full of stray and pet dogs, where a bloody murder, that of their daughter Aarushi had already taken place and already been brought to the attention of the authorities?

The reason Rajesh Talwar implicated Hemraj was because he suspected him and he suspected him because he was missing. There were four people that lived in the house: two remained, one lay murdered and one was missing " Rajesh assumed that the killer was Hemraj. Else, the dentist reasoned to himself, why would he be missing? He could not have imagined at that moment that Hemraj too had been murdered.

The Absence of Visible Grief

An extraordinary number of people told me they believed the Talwars were guilty of murdering their only child because in the aftermath of the killings neither parent appeared to be in the state of grief that was reasonably expected. Parents grieve the loss of a child, and the Talwars' grief would surely have been compounded following the demise of their daughter under such terrible and traumatic circumstances. Celebrity writer and columnist Shobha De stated during a chat show, one of the innumerable that hogged the TV screens for years in the aftermath of Aarushi's murder that the Talwars, especially the mother did not grieve as one would after the death of a child, and that too an only child.

It is not only lay people or celebrities like Shobha De that reasoned thus. Judge Lal who should have had more experience in this matter, and known better, followed similar reasoning. Of his famous twenty-six reasons incorporated in his judgement why the Talwars were guilty beyond reasonable doubt was reason number thirteen, which in his words argued 'that the housemaid Bharti Mandal has nowhere stated that when she came inside the flat both the accused were found weeping'.

It is a bizarre interpretation of a witness's testimony because the maid did *not* state that they were dry-eyed. To interpret from this that they were not weeping is clearly a misrepresentation. If a witness did not state that there was bright sunshine on a particular day, can we interpret from this that there was no sunshine? Furthermore, the CBI Closure Report explicitly states that they *were* weeping. The report clearly stated as follows: '*Dr. Nupur and Dr. Rajesh were found standing in the dining area and opposite the door of Aarushi's room respectively. Both were weeping....*' It is possible that the judge too may have been influenced by the media coverage on the lack of emotion exhibited by the parents following the murder of their only child.

Following the perceived stoniness of the Talwars (more Nupur than Rajesh) a story went around that perhaps Aarushi was not their real daughter. There was even a demand made for a paternity test to ensure that she was their blood. Avirook Sen writes in his book about how Nupur's father explained that it was her temperament, even as a child, to hide her feelings.

A female character in Shakespeare's *Twelfth Night* could not speak of her love because it ran so deep, like 'patience on a monument' but additionally, and more directly on the issue, there are the famous, poignant lines of Elisabeth Barrett Browning in her classic poem *Grief*:

I tell you, hopeless grief is passionless;
That only men incredulous of despair,
Half-taught in anguish, through the midnight air,
Beat upward to God's throne in loud access
Of shrieking and reproach. Full desertness,
In souls as countries lieth silent-bare
Under the blanching, vertical eye-glare
Of the absolute heavens. Deep-hearted man
Express grief for their dead, in silence like to death...

Those who wail and beat their breasts in grief at the passing of a loved one expect others to demonstrate similar physical manifestations of their own extreme emotion. Such persons simply cannot understand, as Browning observes, that there is sometimes a grief that runs so deep the person on whom tragedy has befallen simply falls silent.

Some would still take issue with the notion of quiet grief and point out that if Nupur Talwar had simply fallen silent they could have understood that. She was, however, talking normally, without any visible grief, when she appeared on television for instance. That they say is the point. How could she be so normal? The British are known to be stoic in grief, but Indians are not like that.

Modern day psychologists also talk about the phenomena of extreme grief where the mind simply refuses to absorb the enormity of what has happened; this is a human being's self-defence or coping mechanism. There is quietness, sometimes described as a numbness, in which the mind can carry on as usual, seemingly, while ignoring a reality that it simply cannot fully accept, or absorb. The tears may come much later.

In his essay '*Numbness can be the First Sign of Grief*' clinical psychologist Vijay P. Sharma, writes about this human reaction:

> *Soldiers, with severed limbs, have remained at the front for hours on end without feeling the pain. Numbness is a built-in survival mechanism, perfected over hundreds of thousands of years. The loss of a partner is equally a matter of life and death, threatening our own existence, and invoking our defenses for survival. So the numbness, the inability to feel pain at that moment, enables us to deal with the crisis and gather our forces. The body produces endorphins, a natural morphine to enable us bear those pains and make them manageable. When the pain is unmanageable or too intense to bear, we stop feeling the pain. Numbness is nature's way of buffering pain; this is true for physical as well as emotional pain. In the case of severe 'emotional injury', or shock, a psychological numbness occurs.*
>
> *Many people, when they first hear the news of a loved one's death, they are stunned, unable to cry or feel the pain.*

The authors of *On Grief and Grieving: Finding the Meaning of Grief through the Five Stages of Loss*',[11] a classic treatise on the grieving process write about how denial that the event ever took place is often the first thing that happens.

This first stage of grieving helps us to survive the loss....Denial and shock helps us to cope and make survival possible. Denial helps us to pace our feelings of grief. There is a grace in denial. It is nature's way of letting in only as much as we can handle. These feelings are important; they are the psyche's protective mechanisms. Letting in all the feelings associated with loss would be overwhelming emotionally. We can't believe what has happened because we actually can't believe what has happened. To full believe at this stage would be too much.

Photographic Evidence of Nupur Talwar's Innocence

Aarushi's birthday was only a few days away before her tragic death. According to the statement given by the Talwars (and this has not been disputed by the investigators), Dr Rajesh Talwar had bought a camera online that had already arrived. Nupur convinced her husband that they should give it Aarushi that very evening instead of waiting for her birthday. A typical happy family scenario that most people can identify with soon turned to tragedy. The gift was handed over to an excited Aarushi, who immediately began to take photographs[12]. When investigators examined the camera later, they discovered that several images had been deleted. Suspicions surfaced as to why the deletions had been made[13]; Nupur Talwar pointed out that those were probably just photographs that Aarushi didn't think were so well taken or didn't like and were therefore deleted[14].

The pictures show Rajesh Talwar wearing a red t-shirt, while Nupur is seen in nightclothes. It is a fact full of profound significance that she was found wearing the very same clothes the next morning. The defence team tried to highlight the implications of this during the course of the trial. Judge Shyam Lal was not impressed. In his judgement he acknowledges the facts as stated by the defence:

> *Those photographs which were taken in the evening (show) Dr. Nupur Talwar was also wearing the same gown which she was found wearing in the morning...*[15]

He veers off to discuss how the very same photographs show that someone had dressed up the room after Aarushi's murder, as the positions of various things are different. The argument by the defence is brushed aside with the following words:

> *I am not going to be lured by attractive ingenious and dexterous defence taken by the learned counsel.*

Attractive, ingenious and dexterous...? But clearly not convincing.

He then addresses the issue of Nupur's gown in the following terms:

> *It is also possible that before going to sleep Dr. Nupur Talwar might have changed her gown, which she was wearing at the time of taking pix from digital camera. As stated herein before, being mother of the child it is not possible that on seeing her child dead she would not have hugged her. During hugging certainly, the gown of Dr. Nupur Talwar must have also been blood stained but no blood was found, which clearly shows that she had changed her gown or other night-garment, which she was wearing in the night.*

Let's examine his observations a little more closely.

> *It is also possible that before going to sleep Dr. Nupur Talwar might have changed her gown, which she was wearing at the time of taking pix from digital camera...*

It's certainly possible but theoretically anything is possible. The question is after a day's work Nupur was only going to bed to sleep, and in all likelihood would not have tried on different garments. It is possible indeed, but how likely is it?

> *As stated hereinbefore, being mother of the child it is not possible that on seeing her child dead she would not have hugged her...*

It does start to look here like a case of heads I win, tails you lose. Hereinbefore and hereinafter the judge has been saying other things. Elsewhere in the very same judgement Judge Lal refers to the lack of emotion expressed by Nupur Talwar as a sign of her guilt. Here he states it does not matter that she was wearing the same gown, because 'being mother of the child it is not possible that on seeing her child dead she would not have hugged her'.

The point the defence is making is clear. In the morning when the maid Bharti arrives, Nupur is wearing the same gown as the previous night (as shown in the photographs taken with the camera). Is it possible that that gown would not have carried the blood-stains from Hemraj's body that she is alleged to have carried up the stairs together with her husband? The judge counters this by arguing that it is clear that she must have changed her clothes because as a mother it is simply not possible that she would not have hugged her child. But he doesn't elaborate further. He should have stated that she changed into another garment before hugging her child. How likely is that?

Sending The Police Rushing Off....

The CBI closure report records that '*Dr. Rajesh Talwar had been insisting that the police instead of wasting time in the flat should search for Hemraj*'. The prosecution considered this as suspicious behaviour, because it is argued that Talwar's real intention was to divert the police from searching the terrace. Yes, he was insisting that the police search out Hemraj but that was because he was in a rage and wanted the man who he believed had murdered his daughter apprehended. It was a filial rage that should not be beyond the comprehension of any parent. He didn't wish the police to waste time in the flat and preferred that they used the limited manpower at their disposal towards apprehension of the culprit and not in investigating the matter further. At that point of time he didn't have a shadow of doubt about Hemraj's guilt in the matter.

What was important was to apprehend Hemraj as soon as possible. He may not have gone far. These were the natural thoughts of a father. He was convinced that Hemraj was the killer. And indeed since he was missing, this was not an unnatural assumption.

At that point of time, Rajesh Talwar could not have ever imagined that there was another dead body, that of Hemraj himself, lying in a pool of blood on the terrace.

The Failure to Immediately Identify Hemraj's Body

The way this plays out in the film, said to be true to life is something like this: After a dead body is discovered on the terrace Rajesh Talwar is asked by the NOIDA investigating officer if he can confirm that it is his servant, Hemraj's body. When he sees the body Rajesh Talwar is unable to confirm at once that it is indeed Hemraj.

In the film the policeman says sarcastically: 'He's been working for you for the past two years, and yet you can't recognise him.'

The prosecution was trying to imply that this was a very suspicious circumstance. Rajesh Talwar did not know what to do now. The plan had been to dispose off the body later with the assumption that the police would not find it. He was confused. He didn't want to admit to the police that it was Hemraj's body because Hemraj was the person he had originally held responsible for Aarushi's death. If not Hemraj, then who else? The needle of suspicion would surely now turn to him and his wife and so he hesitated to identify the body as that of Hemraj.

This above scenario seems implausible and underestimates Rajesh Talwar's intelligence even the distraught state in which he was. Had Rajesh Talwar killed Hemraj, he would have instantly realised that others, notably Hemraj's associates Krishna and Rajkumar would be summoned soon enough; the identity of the dead body could not be hidden for long.

So what was the point of stalling and trying to gain time? To what end?

Additionally, there are two further errors in the information provided by the press. Firstly, Hemraj hadn't been working for two years as was reported; it was more like seven to eight months[16]. Secondly, Hemraj's face had bloated enormously after death. The local policeman could not comprehend the extent to which this had happened because he had never seen Hemraj *before* death, so he thought it was the same face. But those who had seen Hemraj before death or those with greater experience understood immediately that the face had altered beyond recognition. Ex-cop Gautam, who was present at the crime scene the morning following the murders, spoke of this. 'It was huge,' Gautam said, using his palms to demonstrate how much the body had swollen '*nobody* was able to recognize him.'[17] Dr Jaising P. Modi's *Textbook of Medical Jurisprudence and Toxicology* also gives out examples of how the appearance can change as '*from 18 to 36 hours or 48 hours after death, eyes are forced out of their sockets, a frothy reddish fluid is forced out of the mouth and nostrils, abdomen becomes greatly distended...*'

In a Hurry for the Cremation....

As per the CBI's closure report (para 13), '*the body of Aarushi was brought back to the residence of Dr. Rajesh Talwar by around 7.30pm. After keeping the body there for about half an hour, the body was taken to the cremation ground in Noida where the last rites of Aarushi were carried out*'.

Could it be argued that Rajesh Talwar's act of cremating Aarushi's body the same day was itself suspicious? It would have indeed been suspicious had Hemraj's body been discovered by then but this was not the case. Till that point in time Rajesh Talwar was fully convinced that Hemraj was the assailant. With the discovery of Hemraj's body the next day, everything changed.

Fingerprints on the Cooler Panel

In the movie *Talvar*, CBI's team one's investigating officer, Arun Kumar sarcastically tells one of the UP policemen that the next time someone leaves a bloodied palm print on the wall, he should take care it doesn't get washed away in the rain. Leaving aside the bloodied handprint on the wall, which was there for the police to see and make a comparison with the prints of the suspects in the case, there would have been fingerprints that were not visible to the naked eye on the cooler panel that was used to cover Hemraj's body. It would not have been a difficult forensic assignment to lift prints off the panel and compare and contrast these with the fingerprints of all the suspects. However, none of those prints were compared. Judge Lal is too forgiving of the investigators when he observes as follows[18]:

> *If the cooler panel has not been taken into possession by S.I. Data Ram Naunaria and he has not directed constable Chunni Lal Gautam to take photographs and finger-prints of panel then it is* ***merely*** *a negligence on the part of Mr. Naunaria but it is well settled law that on account of negligence or defective investigation of I.O. the prosecution case cannot be thrown away or dubbed as untrue and the accused cannot take advantage of the same....*

The Case of the Swollen Penis

The words and statements carry an unnatural, and let it be said, often, unjustified authoritativeness if a person has 'Dr' prefixed to his or her name. The media is not necessarily more discerning than your average person; they too are impressionable. At least that's how it seems to have reported the testimony given by a Dr Raj appearing on behalf of the prosecution who testified that Hemraj's penis was swollen after his death. In his testimony, this particular doctor stated that in his view the reason for this was because Hemraj was either in the middle of sexual intercourse with Aarushi, or was just getting ready to start (i.e. in an aroused state)[19].

Even a non-medical person would scratch his head and be nonplussed on hearing such a testimony coming from the mouth of a registered medical practitioner. Fortunately for the Talwars, their lawyer produced an authoritative medical text that controverted the doctor's testimony. Modi's *Textbook of Medical Jurisprudence and Toxicology* reads as follow:

> *From 18 to 36 hours or 48 hours after death, eyes are forced out of their sockets, a frothy reddish fluid is forced out of the mouth and nostrils, abdomen becomes greatly distended,* ***the penis and scrotum become enormously swollen...***

At this point, the good doctor, Dr Raj could not think of an escape route; indeed he must have quickly realised how foolish it would be for him to try and directly contradict what was in black and white in a medical textbook. If politics is the last refuge of scoundrels, for Dr Raj, it was his marriage that he sought refuge in as the basis for the expert medical opinion he had tendered. This is what he stated in court:

> 'My statement that the reason for swelling found in the penis of the deceased Hemraj was that he was murdered either while he was in the midst of sexual intercourse or just before commencing intercourse is based on my marriage and experience of my marriage....I cannot produce any authority in support of my statement.'[20]

What could Dr Raj have possibly meant by his extraordinary and outlandish statement is not elaborated any further. He could have said his medical studies had led him to form such and such conclusion; previous post-mortems had led him to form this opinion; he could even have tried to contradict the authoritative medical text produced before him (though that would have been difficult) but his experience with his own marriage – what on earth did this mean? If one were to hazard a guess, it would be something not very dissimilar to the following imaginary conversation between two 'less well informed' readers of the reports that appeared in the media. Let's call them A and B.

A: Did you see the report in the papers today? It's now clear that the servant Hemraj *was* having sex with the fourteen-year-old girl that got killed.

B: How can they be so sure?

A: Oh, didn't you read? The expert doctor who had conducted the post-mortem discovered that the servant's penis was swollen.

B: Do you mean an erection?

A: Not really. You know once you experience an erection, even after the excitement has passed your penis doesn't immediately shrink back to normal... It remains kind of swollen...

B: I see.

A: At least that's always been the case with me. You're not married so you don't know....*I have discovered this during the course of my marriage (just like the doctor did).*

B: Possibly you are right, but has this happened to you even after experiencing sudden fear? Now, wouldn't Hemraj have seen the doctor getting ready to attack him and immediately lost his erection out of fear?

A: That may not have necessarily happened. You do have a point about the fear element, but he may not have immediately lost an erection (*thinking*). Hemraj may not even have seen Rajesh Talwar. Perhaps the doctor may have attacked him so suddenly and quickly that his penis didn't have the time to react. Don't forget the brain has to send a signal to the penis.

B: On the other hand, when Hemraj was hit with the golf club, wouldn't the pain have caused him to lose his erection completely? You were speaking about what you have learnt from your marriage.

Has your wife ever hit you hard during intercourse and you've still been able to maintain your erection?

A: No, that has never happened. Don't forget this is an expert doctor's testimony and he happens to agree with me.

B: But, surely after his death...

B: You know rigor mortis sets in. Everything gets kind of frozen into place...

A: How soon is that?

And the conversation continues so on and forth....

To the readers who object to the above, I ask that they provide an alternative explanation of what Dr Raj could possibly have meant when he said he discovered something about swollen penises during the course of his marriage.

What did the judge make of all this?

On page 105 of his judgement, Judge Shyam Lal compares the testimony of the doctor appearing for the prosecution with the testimony of the doctor for the defence in fairly garbled language. It takes a second, or third, reading before it makes any sense. The judge writes about the case of Hemraj's swollen penis in these terms:

> *Dr. Naresh Raj* (witness for the prosecution) *has mentioned in his postmortem examination report that the penis of Hemraj was found swollen but if he has stated before the court that the swelling was because either he had been murdered in the midst of sexual intercourse or just before he was about to have sexual intercourse is nothing but quite preposterous and really a medical blasphemy as the reasons ascribed by him are ludicrous.*
>
> *Dr. R.K. Sharma* (witness for the defence) *has rightly pointed out in his statement that in the post-mortem examination report of Hemraj, Dr. Naresh Raj has written that eyes were protruding out; blood oozing out of mouth and nostrils, stomach was distended and there was*

swelling in the penis which are all signs of putrification and therefore, swelling in the penis and scrotum was an account of putrification of the dead body and not because of sexual intercourse.

Be that as it may, the fact remains that the penis of Hemraj was found swollen at the time of post-mortem examination of his dead body.

More contradictions. On the one hand, the judge quite rightly dismissed the suggestion that the swollen state of Hemraj's penis had anything to do with preparatory or on-going sexual activity at the time of his murder. He even terms it 'medical blasphemy'. At the same time, as if he himself isn't so clear on this point he intriguingly adds:

'***Be that as it may,*** *the fact remains that the penis of Hemraj was found swollen at the time of post-mortem examination of his dead body.'*

One is tempted to add: be that as it may the fact remains it was completely unnecessary for the judge to make this extra noting with regards to Hemraj's swollen penis.

Was the Vagina Dilated or Closed?

The world of medicine, like that of law, is vast, so much so that a fully qualified doctor could depose on 'medical observations' that may directly contradict what an expert in the field might profess.

A gynaecologist would know more about the behaviour of female sexual organs before and after death than would a doctor lacking such expertise with the female body. One would, however, expect that general practitioners would cross check their facts and so-called observations, for depositions in court are serious business, especially in the context of a murder trial. Clearly, sometimes they do not bother to do so.

Dr Sunil Dohre conducted the post-mortem on Aarushi. The post-mortem report did not state *anything* about the vagina being dilated.

In a statement to the police in October 2008, widely reported in the media and accepted as fact by the general public or those without specialist knowledge, Dr Sunil Dohre stated that the vagina was so dilated that he could even see the cervix.[21]

In his deposition before the court he maintained that the vagina was abnormally dilated but by then he could no longer see the cervix, or at least did not state that it could be seen.

Those who support the case for the dentist couple's innocence might suggest that he had researched the issue and found it would be nothing short of miraculous; he would have needed x-ray vision to be able to see the cervix.

An important question surfaces here. Why did Dr Dohre not mention the state of the vagina in his post-mortem report? The investigating officer of CBI team two asked him this very question in court, so one can assume that he may have had time to ponder his response.

This is how that Q & A went.[22]

Kaul: During your examination you have found certain peculiar facts about the private parts of the body but the same have not been mentioned in the PM (post mortem) report. Why?

Dohre: Comments about the private parts of the body were not made as the findngs were non-specific and were very strange.

The findings were non-specific and were very strange... said the doctor.

Firstly, how were they non-specific? The vagina was dilated, what is non-specific about this?

The findings were... very strange...

If the findings were strange this was all the more reason to ensure that those details should have been mentioned in the post mortem report. Why should 'strange findings' be excluded? What does the doctor think a post-mortem is about? It is precisely meant to find out 'strange' things. If a death is considered natural, a post-mortem isn't conducted. The response, despite being prepared, is deeply unsatisfactory.

Let us now see how Judge Lal responds to Dr Dohre's excuse.

The judge is happy to overlook the fact that the initial post mortem report did not make certain observations with respect to the vaginal cavity. He considers this discrepancy unimportant and observes:

> *If Dr. Dohre has not mentioned in the post-mortem examination report that opening of vaginal cavity was prominent and the vaginal canal was visible; that the vaginal orifice of Aarushi was wide and open and that vaginal canal could be seen; that the hymen of the deceased was old, torn and healed and these facts were not stated to the earlier investigating officers on 18.05.2008, 18.07.2008 and 03.10.2008 then it cannot be said that his statement cannot be relied upon.* ***Since questions regarding the condition of vagina were not specifically asked by the earlier investigating officers and therefore, there was no occasion to tell about these facts to them*** *(sic).*

'There was no occasion to tell about these facts to them', is what the judge writes. Aside from the unimportant grammatical error 'tell about these facts' this statement by the judge appears to suggest, against all common sense and logic that a post mortem report should be as concise as possible, and the report (just like the vagina itself?) should be expanded only if there are specific queries from investigating officers. This is bizarre reasoning coming from a seasoned judge. Elsewhere in the judgement, Judge Lal lauds the extensive experience and seniority of

Dr Dohre. If the good doctor was indeed so experienced and knowledgeable, shouldn't he have known that post mortem reports should be as comprehensive as possible? Does Judge Shyam Lal really believe that it was the duty of the investigating officers to prompt the doctor as to the size of the vaginal cavity, etc?

The case of the swollen penis referred to earlier obviously needed some complementarity. One the one hand, you have the swollen penis and on the other, a dilated vagina. Two plus two makes twenty goes this strange logic and so this state of the sexual organs is proof in the eyes of less informed individuals that there was sexual intercourse taking place at, or near, the time the killings took place. And so to continue with our make believe conversation between our two fictitious characters:

B: What you say about the penis remaining swollen because Hemraj was engaged in sexual intercourse makes sense...but I have a question here. Would not Aarushi's vagina also remain dilated assuming that she was killed within a few seconds of Hemraj being killed?

A: (thinking hard) As a matter of fact you are right. Her vagina should be extremely dilated, especially since she was such a young girl.

B: So, I take it then that this was consensual sex?

A: Of course. If it hadn't been consensual there would have been no reason for Dr Talwar to kill his daughter. What more proof do we need that sex was taking place? The servant's swollen penis, on the one hand and Aarushi's dilated vagina, on the other.

B: Both so convenient from the point of proving that there was sex happening in the room. Case closed.

Someone with expert knowledge countered the doctor's testimony. Dr Urmila Sharma, a trained and experienced gynaecologist who appeared for the defence, asserted that after death the vaginal canal could not be visible unless the examiner used an instrument.[23]

This testimony cleared assailed Dr Dohre's report. The prosecution's counsel was therefore compelled to ask Dr Sharma if the vagina of the girl would not remain dilated if she 'is used to sexual intercourse and her vagina is cleaned after her death'.

Dr Urmila Sharma was categorical in her response. 'The mouth of the vagina will still not remain open,' she asserted.

Clearly at a loss, counsel for the prosecution tries to save his position by then asking what would happen if force was used after rigor mortis.

Dr Urmila Sharma agreed that in those circumstances the vagina could remain open or dilated, but there would necessarily be injury marks. There was, however, no mention of any injuries in that area in either the post mortem report or in subsequent reports provided by Dr Sunil Dohre.

One doesn't have to be a gynaecologist or even a medical professional to be convinced of the assertions made by Dr Urmila Sharma.

Rigor mortis can set in between two and six hours after death. It involves a stiffening of the muscles. The body loses its flaccidity. In this state body parts cannot be manipulated without causing injury.

I would rank both possibilities in order of their likelihood.

1. The vagina was *not* dilated. Dr Dohre, who carried out the post mortem, did not observe the extraordinary dilation of the vagina. After all, he did not make this observation in his post mortem report. Later, in his statement to the police in October 2008 he went over the top and stated that the vagina was so dilated that he could see the

cervix – a medical impossibility. Subsequent statements did not make any further mention of the cervix being visible.

2. The vagina was indeed dilated, suggesting a clean up after rigor mortis. This seems unlikely. As Dr Urmila Sharma explained, in order for vaginal dilation to be sustained the clean up could have only taken place after rigor mortis had set in. However, this couldn't have been possible without causing injuries in the area. No injuries were noted. Therefore it was unlikely that the vagina was dilated. However, for the sake of argument, let's assume the prosecution and Dr Dohre are right in both respects: firstly, that the vagina was dilated and secondly, it was the Talwars who had cleaned it up. The injuries though minor in nature were very much there and were either overlooked or were simply not noticed because the examination was not as careful and minute as it should have been. But there is still a problem with this hypothesis. The problem is the prosecution alleged that the killings took place because Rajesh Talwar found Aarushi in a compromising position with the servant. If this were the case, would he then wait two hours for rigor mortis to set in before doing the clean up? On the other hand, if Aarushi had been assaulted and killed by someone else it is theoretically possible that by the time the Talwars woke up in the morning, rigor mortis had already set in and the clean up was done then. That would, however, mean they were not the killers.

Was the Vagina Dilated Because of Intercourse or Cleaning the Area After the Killing?

As stated earlier, the dilation of the vagina was never mentioned in the post mortem report. It was only much later that the doctor deposed that this had been the case. The confused logic that emerges from the so-called dilated vagina represents a two-pronged argument against the Talwars. The first of these, although not articulated, is a sly suggestion that the vagina was dilated because Aarushi was engaged in sexual intercourse (The question by the prosecution's counsel to the medical expert appearing for the defence was whether it would not remain dilated if Aarushi was *'used to sexual intercourse* and her vagina is cleaned after her death'.

This suggestion was strongly refuted by Dr Urmila Sharma. The second argument for the prosecution was that even if it was true that the vagina resumes its normal shape after intercourse, it could have been dilated if there had been cleaning up and manipulation after death.

The medical fact is that the vaginal cavity does not remain dilated after intercourse, no matter how vigorous it may have been. The prosecution's question was senseless. If it does not remain dilated after intercourse, why would it remain dilated after manipulation? After all, it can be argued that sexual intercourse is itself a kind of manipulation.

The prosecution continued to labour the point and assert that the vagina had been manipulated and cleaned up by the Talwars. Even here there is clear contradiction, for it was not really cleaned up, was it? In the very same breath the prosecution speaks of a whitish discharge from the vagina. If the vagina had indeed been cleaned up the question needs to be raised: wherefrom did this whitish discharge appear? What indeed was the point of the so-called cleaning and manipulation of the vagina if the discharge, which was not even stuck to the walls of the vagina but was easily visible hadn't been cleaned up? In fact the presence of the whitish discharge suggested rather clearly that the vagina had NOT been cleaned up. It was only the pubic area from the outside that had been cleaned up.

Despite the crudity of the arguments and depositions, there is subtle psychological play at work here; it is somehow being hinted that that whitish substance could have been Hemraj's semen, but it is a matter of forensic record that no traces of semen were found. So we have a somewhat incredible, if not downright fantastic, scenario in which we have a swollen penis, a dilated vagina the combination clearly suggestive to the lay newspaper devouring public that sexual intercourse had taken place. The third, semen that would have served as an absolute confirmation is, however, missing. That would have been difficult to manufacture, although there has been an incident of a rape case recorded in India, in the days when forensic science was in its infancy where a policeman used his own semen on female clothing to buttress an allegation of rape against an accused.

Of course it is possible for sexual intercourse to have taken place even if semen is not found as the judge suggested, but in the 'cleaning up and manipulation' argument advanced by the prosecution, it somewhat deviously and foolishly suggests an explanation for *why* it was missing. It was missing, you see, because the vagina had been cleaned up, and the evidence that there had been a 'clean up' is the dilated vagina, but then the further questions that arise are conveniently ignored. How were the Talwars able to clean up the semen and not the whitish discharge? From where did that whitish discharge appear? It's no one's case that the whitish discharge could have taken place after the murder.

What did Judge Shyam Lal have to say about the whitish discharge?

That Whitish Discharge

There is one other glaring contradiction within the judgement that leaps up from the pages. The judge, somewhat bizarrely concludes despite expert gynaecological evidence to the contrary that the whitish discharge from the vagina proves that Aarushi was engaged in sexual intercourse. This is simply not true medically speaking. The judge phrased it thus:

Unequivocally, white discharge was found in the vaginal cavity of Ms. Aarushi at the time of post-mortem examination of her dead body by Dr. Sunil Kumar Dohre and this fact has not been gainsaid by the accused persons in their statements.... ***Presence of white discharge in the vaginal cavity of Ms. Aarushi denotes that she was engaged in sexual intercourse, albeit, no spermatozoa were found in the vaginal swab.***

I did a double take when I came across this paragraph in the judgement and read it a second time to make sure that I was not mistaken. This is an incompletely unscientific and unwarranted inference made by the judge. Does the presence of a whitish discharge in the vagina of a teenage girl indicate she'd been having sex? I know that Judge Lal has a son but uncertain if he has daughters. He needs to know that a whitish discharge in teenage girls is a completely normal gynaecological occurrence and has nothing to do with having sex.

This is what Kathy McCoy and Charles Wibbelsman, two experts on the teenage body have to say[24]:

'It's normal to have a clear, whitish non irritating vaginal discharge. This mixture of mucus, bacteria and discarded vaginal cells may turn from clear or white to pale yellow as it is exposed to the air'.

No sperm was found in the vaginal swab, but this too is dismissed the judge as unimportant. Another 'mere' emerges. The whitish discharge is proof that sex was taking place. This is what he has to say with respect to the absence of semen:[25]

Mere absence of spermatozoa in the vaginal swab cannot rule out possibility of sexual intercourse.

The Severing of an Artery

According to Dr Raj, who deposed on behalf of the prosecution, the injury to Hemraj's neck was caused by 'a very sharp edged light instrument'[26]. Reported widely in the press, for many this was conclusive proof that the Talwars had murdered their daughter and servant.

A very sharp edged light instrument...

A weapon used to sever an artery has necessarily to be very sharp, so no great deductions here. However, the crucial bit in this part of the statement is the word 'light'.

This would seem to exclude a butcher's knife, a big kitchen knife or a khukri, as these objects may be very sharp but are certainly not light. This conclusion was further fortified when Dr Raj went on to refer to 'the identical position of the injury and the skill with which the cut is made....'

A few questions surface.

Is it beyond the realms of possibility that Dr Raj made his statement in that particular way, referring to the lightness of the weapon and also implying that it may have been an 'instrument,' and thus giving his deposition a certain slant at the behest of the CBI? After all, a high level medical committee from the All India Institute of Medical Sciences (AIIMS) did conclude earlier that cuts inflicted by a khukri would have been consistent with the nature of injuries sustained on the neck of the two deceased and was therefore a credible weapon. A khukri is certainly not a light instrument. Before we permit ourselves to allow Dr Raj's deposition to override the conclusions of the AIIMS committee we need to remind ourselves that this is the same physician who, when cornered on the question of how the swollen penis of a dead man could lead him to conclude that the person had been having sex, or was about to commence the act, countered weakly with the assertion that his conclusions were based 'on his marriage'.

Secondly, even if we assume what Dr Raj stated is the truth, as he saw it, is it beyond possible that Krishna, the compounder who had been training for some years now and would have assisted the doctor couple on dental surgeries on numerous occasions could have deliberately inflicted the wounds in order to seek revenge and implicate Dr Rajesh Talwar who had publicly humiliated him only the previous week? How difficult is it to make a precise cut to the neck once you have seen precision in action over the course of many years in dental surgeries? Was Rajesh Talwar foolish enough to not know that using a precise surgical instrument instead of a kitchen knife would obviously implicate him and his wife in the murders?

On the other hand, as far as Hemraj's associates were concerned there were good reasons why the incisions to the neck were necessary. They wanted to be sure that Aarushi was dead, and this was the best way to be certain beyond any doubt. They could not feel her breath, but leaving her alive would be too risky. They had to make sure that she was dead. Could they not have simply bludgeoned her to death (she was already near-dead, said the prosecution) or even strangled her? Moreover, if she was still alive strangling her might cause her to scream. Continuing to bludgeon her would inevitably create a noise that had the possibility of waking up her parents sleeping in the next room. Severing the artery guaranteed that the victim would be dead. It would be a noiseless crime that would not awaken anyone (even if it was messy).

If Wounds Could Speak What Would They Say

The Post-Mortem

With respect to Aarushi's post-mortem, Judge Shyam Lal noted:

> *Dr. Sunil Kumar Dohre, Medical Officer, Incharge of Primary Health Centre, Sector 22, NOIDA conducted autopsy on the cadaver of Ms. Aarushi between 12.00 o' clock in the noon till 01:30 P.M. The deceased was aged about 14 years; rigor mortis was present in both*

upper limb and lower limb. She was average built, both eyes were congested. Whitish discharge was found in the vagina.[27]

Judge Lal then goes on to describe the injuries. Aside from the injuries to the neck there were two injuries that he referred to. She had a wound measuring 4cmx3cm just one centimetre above her left eye on her brow that entered into her skull's cavity. There was also a wound on the left parietal region.[28] Two wounds then, although the Talwars' lawyers maintained there was only one.[29]

Dr Naresh Raj carried out the post-mortem on Hemraj. Judge Lal cited the report as recording that 'the deceased was aged about 45 years and average built.' It went on to state that 'his (Hemraj's) eyes were protruding bilaterally. Bleeding from nostril and mouth was seen. Penis was swollen'.

Abrasions

With respect to the injuries found on Hemraj's person there were several abrasions, which were not found on Aarushi's body. There was an abrasion 'measuring 3 cm. x 2 cm behind the right elbow' and a similar abrasion measuring '3 cm. x 4 cm. behind the left elbow'. There were two more abrasions on the left frontal region, one measuring 2cmx2cm and the other 3cmx2cm above the left eyebrow.

The presence of these abrasions was used to support the theory advanced by the prosecution that Hemraj's body was carried up the staircase by the Talwars; on the other hand, those same abrasions could have been caused by Hemraj's associates carrying his body across the terrace to a suitable spot where it would not be easily detected from the neighbouring terrace. As a matter of fact the CBI Closure Report states: '*As soon as the door was opened, all those present saw that there were blood marks on the roof as if a body as been dragged*'.

The Incisions

As regards the incisions on the neck they were similar in nature; however, the cut made on Hemraj's neck was much longer than the cut made on Aarushi's neck. The location of the wound is described as follows: 'The wound was 30 cms long and is situated 5 cm. below right ear, 6 cm below left ear and 6 cm below the chin'. At fourteen centimetres the incision made on Aarushi's neck is less than half the length.

Aarushi's left carotid artery was slit and her blood was all over, but as far as Hemraj's blood was concerned, not one single drop was detected. In a killing as bloody as this one, this 'special circumstance' or fact, call it what you will, would completely rule out the possibility that Hemraj's artery was severed in the same room. The explanation provided by the NOIDA police investigators was that the Talwars had cleaned it all up, just as they had dressed up the room. Dressing up the room is one thing, removing all traces of Hemraj's blood a completely different ball game.

In fact in the film *Talvar*, Arun Kumar played by Irrfan Khan sarcastically tells the policeman from UP in not so many words: 'So, I understand that the blood of Aarushi was red and that of Hemraj was green and that's why it was so easy for the parents to clean it up, wasn't it?' He could have also phrased it in these terms: despite the maniacal attack that ensued (according to the prosecution) with Talwar completely off his rockers, the attack took place in such a manner that Hemraj's blood fell in a neat little puddle by the side somewhere clearly demarcated and quite separate from Aarushi's blood which fell into a separate puddle (on the other side of the bed?) And that's the simple reason why it was so easy to clean it all up...

Rajesh Talwar, the Golfer Par Excellence

No injuries were found on other parts of either Aarushi's or Hemraj's bodies. The theory of sudden blind rage doesn't sit very well with just two or three finely calibrated hits with a golf club. The blunt injury was inflicted on Aarushi on her forehead above the left eye. Hemraj received a blow on the back of his head. Had there been a few more injuries the golf club theory could have still held some credence.

Rajesh Talwar must have been a golfer par excellence so much so that in a single swing of the club he hit the right spot on Hemraj's head and thereafter on Aarushi's head.

Assuming for a moment that the scenario of Aarushi and Hemraj being caught having sex was true, but upon sensing Rajesh Talwar's presence or seeing him enter they would have tried to protect themselves from blows, and would have necessarily sustained other injuries. Instead they are both killed practically on the first or second blow. It is also unbelievable that Aarushi and Hemraj not only left the bedroom door ajar (as stated by the investigating officer in court), they also did not hear Rajesh Talwar shout for Hemraj or indeed enter the room.

The other point is that unlike other heavy objects (bricks, blocks of iron, etc.) it is commonsensical that a golf club cannot really kill someone unless you can have a proper swing. What makes Rajesh Talwar's performance still more impressive is that he was able to execute two deaths with two or three swings, an average of almost one death per swing. (Although the prosecution spoke of two injuries, the Talwars' lawyers insisted that there was only a single injury).[30] To make this feat still more impressive, it was accomplished in a room that did not really provide him with much 'swing room'. The prosecution raised the possibility of swingless killings during the course of the cross examination of a witness. 'Swingless' killings do happen, but in those cases the killing weapon cannot be a golf club. It is certainly possible to hammer a person to death, and a hammer doesn't need a full swing, but a partial 'throw back' is probable. It is not possible to use a golf club as a hammer, and in any case it doesn't fit the sudden rage scenario. Would the prosecution have Rajesh Talwar enter the room with a golf club and then sit next to Aarushi and Hemraj and use the club like a hammer – with them just sitting back and taking it?

No room for a proper swing, and despite the fury that is said to have gripped him, Rajesh Talwar was apparently still calm enough to execute these swings with near perfect precision (it would of course have been more impressive if he had been able to kill two birds with one stone, or to have, in other words killed both the servant and his daughter with a single swing).

The Cleanest of the Clubs

We must also not forget to applaud CBI Team Two and the prosecution for deducing and convincing Judge Shyam Lal that it must have been the cleanest of the golf clubs that was used for the killing. Not the most helpful in executing a killing, nothing to do with 'weapon of choice' of course. What if the putter had been the cleanest?

Judge Shyam Lal himself was clearly not a golfer else he would not have referred to golf clubs as golf 'sticks' which he does on several occasions.[31] However, even non-golfers understand that players will use certain clubs more than others and will, for this reason have more soil on them. The soil deposit on a golf club is not, however, a mere function of how frequently it is used but also in what circumstances it is used. For example, if you are planning a long hit, you have a choice between a few clubs that are appropriate for the distance, and when you go in for an ambitious hard stroke that is likely to push up more soil – especially if you miss the target. What is certain is that the deposit of soil on a golf club, or its absence, scarcely proves anything, and most certainly not which was the weapon of a murder.

And yet this is the kind of reasoning put forward by the CBI and accepted by the court. The CBI reasoned that the murder weapon would have been cleaned up and therefore would have had less soil deposited on it. The cleanest golf club would therefore be the murder weapon.

QED

The court accepted the 'clean' golf club argument because of a broad correspondence between the dimensions of the injury with the shape of the club. On the question of dimensions of the injuries sustained, a hockey stick would have had pretty much the same result. There could, additionally, be numerous objects that could have caused similar sized injuries.

The judge also accepted the dental scalpel proposal despite the alleged weapon not being recovered, and simultaneously rubbished the report of a high level AIIMS Committee comprising highly qualified medical personnel which had concluded in its report submitted to the previous investigating officer of the CBI that the injuries *could* have been caused by a khukri. It was not just one expert but also a committee of experts that came to this conclusion. Were they lying or under kind pressure to have submitted such a report?

Without addressing those questions, Judge Shyam Lal observed rather astonishingly as follows: '*In view of this clinching scientific evidence, it is conclusively proved that lacerated wounds of both the deceased were caused by golf stick. The incised wounds of both the deceased are of same pattern and cannot be caused by khukri and rather possible to have been caused by a small sharp-edged instrument like scalpel. In view of above findings it can safely be concluded that injuries as mentioned above were caused by golf club and scalpel.*'

A few expressions jump out and assail the better-informed reader, such as '...*cannot* be caused by *khukri*' and '*clinching* scientific evidence' leaving no scope for doubt or error. So clearly the judge knows better than the experts.

The 'Discovery' of the Murder Weapons

The judgement somehow implies that Rajesh Talwar had hidden the golf club because it was the murder weapon. Normally, even if the weapon itself is not discovered, it can be expected that the nature of a murder weapon is identified soon after the killing or at least within a few weeks or months after the crime. Here the 'discovery' of the golf club, the alleged murder weapon took a year and a half. The truth of the matter is that the delay in the discovery of the murder weapon was not because Rajesh Talwar had hidden it. As a matter of fact, it was Rajesh who himself handed over the golf club, the so-called murder weapon, to the investigators. Any delay in 'discovery' took place because the idea that a golf club was the murder weapon occurred to the prosecution years after the crime!

The delays in the trial played out to the advantage of the prosecution and to the extreme disadvantage of the Talwars. In most developed countries (and India is aspiring to become one) criminal trials are continued within a year and a half of the occurrence of a crime. In this case as pointed out by the defence from '16.05.2008 to October 2009 (i.e. for a year and a half) the golf club was never in the spectrum of the investigating agencies'[32]. It was a late 'brainwave', if it can be called that, on part of A.G.L. Kaul, the new investigating officer who headed CBI Team Two. It was also pointed out by the defence that it was *two* years after the murders that, 'Dr. Dohre **for the first time** on 28.05.2010 gave statement to the I.O. that blunt injuries were caused by a golf club'.[33]

For that matter even the 'surgical scalpel' was a late invention. This was the second killing weapon that the prosecution proposed. As acknowledged by the judge, 'Dr. Dohre has nowhere stated on 18.05.2008, 18.07.2008 and 03.10.2008 that injury nos. 2 and 4 (the injuries on the neck) may be caused by surgically sharp-edged weapon and for the first time he has stated before the investigation officer on 30.09.2009 and 28.05.2010 that injury nos. 2 and 4 were caused by sharp-edged surgical instrument'.

Unlike the golf club the dentist's scalpel was never recovered or produced. Two related questions surface. Would Dr Rajesh Talwar keep a surgical scalpel in his house, considering that its frequent use did not fall within his dental speciality? Although the possibility cannot be completely ruled out, wasn't this something he would keep at his clinic instead? Without these two inventions, the golf club and the surgical scalpel, which created a false but impressive visual of the crime, it would have been difficult to pin the crime on to the Talwars.

Neither of the Talwars were regular users of a scalpel in their dental work. Dr Rajesh Talwar was qualified in prosthodontics; the surgical scalpel is really used only by orthodontists, a distinct speciality. Instead of the prosecution having to prove that a dental scalpel *was* used to sever the arteries of the victims, the Talwars had to prove that such an instrument was *not* used.

A witness for the defence Dr Amulya Chaddha, a dentist and professor stated in his deposition that '*normally in injuries caused by scalpels one is bound to see slashes and injuries on the necks of the deceased (which) do not have the pattern of slashes and rather they are deep which can be caused by heavy sharp-edged and curved shaped weapon*'.[34]

Judge Shyam Lal rejected this opinion furnished on behalf of the defence observing grandly that '*(t)he court is not bound by the opinions of the doctors, because after all medical evidence is basically opinionative and is of advisory character. The opinion of a doctor cannot be treated as gospel truth and last word*'.[35]

Medical evidence is basically opinionative and is of advisory character....

The opinion of a doctor cannot be treated as gospel truth and last word....

I reproduce the above observations in the judgement for the reader to react as he wishes to....

A final question arises. Why would the Talwars use a dental scalpel even if one were miraculously available at hand? A kitchen knife could have been used instead. The dental scalpel does not also somehow fit the notion of a crime of sudden rage for it requires a certain attentiveness that is not the hallmark of most crimes of sudden rage.

A Day is Only Twelve Hours, said the Good Doctor

If one were to believe Dr Sunil Dohre, the good doctor who conducted the post mortem, Aarushi actually died while at school that day, and may be an apparition returned home, received the promised camera from her loving parents and was later murdered in her bedroom.

I make the above remarks facetiously, but also with anger, because Dr Dohre's carelessness bordered on irresponsibility when he wrote in the post mortem report that Aarushi had died a day or a day and a half earlier. Judge Shyam Lal is, however, more forgiving and refers to this episode in the following terms[36]:

The penultimate submission of the learned counsel for the accused is that Dr. Dohre has mentioned in his report that the time of the death of Ms. Aarushi is 1 to 1, 1/2 days from the time of conducting the postmortem examination but in the court he has stated that time of death was 12-18 hours from the time of conducting postmortem examination....

I agree with this contention to the extent that Dr. Dohre has incorrectly mentioned in his report that the time of death of Ms. Aarushi was 1 to 1, 1/2 days from the time of conducting postmortem examination and one day is of only 12 hours. ***This court fails to understand as to why this gentleman has stated that one day is of only 12 hours.*** *However, the remaining part of his evidence cannot be brushed aside on that ground.*

Elsewhere in the judgement, Dr Dohre's background, experience and testimonials come in for high praise from the judge. While it is true, as Judge Lal observes 'that falsity of a particular material would not be vitiate the entire testimony of the witness concerned' does the doctor provide an explanation for such a serious lapse? Here is how the judge receives the explanation in the tones of an indulgent parent:

When he (Dr Dohre) was questioned by the court itself as to how this time was written by him then he stated that the deceased had died about 12 o'clock in the night and he had conducted postmortem examination at about 12 o'clock in the noon and when he was going to complete the postmortem examination report then media persons came there and therefore the time of Ms. Aarushi's death as 1 to 11/2 days ***was written down in haste****. It is worthwhile to mention here that both the accused have not taken the plea that death of Ms. Aarushi did not take place in the mid-night and therefore if any blunder has been committed by Dr. Dohre while recording the time of death of Ms. Aarushi in the postmortem examination report then no benefit can be derived by the accused.*

Extending himself unnecessarily as if in a condonation of the absurdity the judge goes on to remark on how *'it is also important to mention here that exact time of death cannot be stated with mathematical accuracy by any doctor conducting postmortem examination and there can be variation of 3 to 4 hours on either side of death.'*

Where was Hemraj's Throat Slit – Bedroom or the Terrace?

While Judge Lal is confident that the throats of both Aarushi and Hemraj were slit using a dental scalpel, and rules against the possibility of any other weapon he is not so clear on where the final execution of Hemraj was carried out. This is definitely one of the important links in the chain of events that needed to be established by the prosecution in order to sustain a conviction.

I read Judge Shyam Lal's lengthy verdict thrice to see if he categorically stated anywhere that he agreed with the testimony given by A.G.L. Kaul that Hemraj received injuries caused only by a blunt instrument in Aarushi's room, and that the carotid artery inside his neck was severed on the terrace.

Judge Lal's verdict is a masterpiece of obfuscation in this and other important aspects. Nowhere in his verbose judgement does he make his opinion on this matter patently known: was Hemraj's artery cut while he was in Aarushi's room or after he was taken to the terrace? It would therefore seem that he considers both scenarios possible. While A.G.L. Kaul, investigating officer, CBI Team Two clearly stated that the Talwars took Hemraj's body to the terrace, and it was there that the artery was slit, when the state police investigated the matter they believed that his artery was slit in Aarushi's room itself and later the bloodied body was taken upstairs.

The question remains: Even if the judge considers both scenarios to be possible, which does he consider to be *more* plausible? Judge Shyam Lal does not answer this essential question. There is only a throwaway clause, as the expression goes, where he observes that '*It is* ***also possible*** *that after bludgeoning Hemraj with golf stick he was carried in a bed sheet by both the accused to the terrace when he was in a state of concussion and thereafter on the terrace his throat was slit and body was dragged*'.[37]

From this it could be interpreted that the judge considered it more likely that the state police was correct in this regard and the artery was severed in Aarushi's room (though with not any degree of finality since the judge is not always precise in the use of his expressions).

As the Supreme Court ruled in the case of *Dharam Das Wadhwani versus State of UP,* a case incidentally cited by the judge, each link in the chain of circumstances has to be properly established. The court observed how 'Link after link, forged firmly by credible testimony may form a strong chain of sure guilt binding the accused....'

Where are those links? And are they clearly established as required? The judge is not even clear in his mind where the incisions to Hemraj's neck were made, but he states that he is completely confident (i.e beyond all reasonable doubt) that the Talwars were the killers.

Is this vagueness accidental or deliberate? Of course if the judge was to make a clear and positive assertion that yes, both Aarushi's and Hemraj's arteries were severed in the teenager's bedroom, he would then be hard put to explain how not a drop of Hemraj's blood was found in the bedroom. Is it perhaps for this reason that he has chosen to remain deliberately vague on this matter?

Blood on the Staircase

It is therefore all the more surprising that Judge Shyam Lal makes such a fuss about blood being found on the staircase. It is as if the blood would tell its own tale. It may well do under certain circumstances but the Aarushi case is not one of them. The judge does not explain anywhere how the presence, or absence, of blood on the staircase rules out the fact that the killers could have been someone else and how this fact alone implicates the Talwars in any way.

Two witnesses spoke about there being blood on the staircase on the morning Aarushi's dead body was discovered. Judge Lal notes that this is evidence given by two doctors who are known to Dr Rajesh Talwar and would therefore have no reason to depose against him. But were they really deposing against him? Let us read it in the judge's own words:[38]

Dr. Rajiv Kumar Varshney has also testified that on receiving a message about the murder of Ms. Aarushi he went there at about 9.00 am but by mistake he climbed up to the terrace door where in the door and lock he found blood stains and then he located the flat of Dr. Rajesh Talwar and came inside where Dr. Rohit Kochar and his wife met him to whom he told about the presence of blood stains on door and lock of the terrace. Thereupon, he came with Dr. Rohit Kochar near the terrace door and showed him blood stains.

He has further stated that ***on minute observation*** *blood stains were seen in the stairs.* ***Meanwhile, a policeman also came there and he was also shown the blood stains on the stairs....***

A bit further the judge notes:

Dr. Rohit Kochar was also the colleague of Dr. Rajesh Talwar in ITS Dental College, NOIDA and since 2007 he was acquainted with Dr. Rajesh Talwar, he has deposed that on 16.05.2008 at about 8.00-8.15 am he received a telephone call from one friend who informed him about the murder of Ms. Aarushi and then he along with his wife Dr. Preeti Kochar went to the house of Dr. Rajesh Talwar where a large number of persons were present there. After about 45-60 minutes Dr. Rajiv Kumar Varshney came there and told him that by mistake he had gone up to the terrace door and had witnessed blood stains on handle of terrace door and floor and then he went up with him and found foot prints of red colour which appear to have been cleaned and blood stains on the handle of terrace door. He has also stated that by that time some persons also came there ***and one of them was a policeman****, who was also shown the bloodstains.*

It may be useful to extract a couple of clauses from the above testimony:

Meanwhile, a policeman also came there and he was also shown the blood stains on the stairs....

And, with respect to the testimony of the second witness:

He has also stated that by that time some persons also came there ***and one of them was a policeman****, who was also shown the bloodstains.*

If the above testimony demonstrates anything at all, it is only how careless the police was in not having the lock to the terrace broken and entering the terrace where they would have immediately discovered Hemraj's dead body. Nothing in the above testimony even remotely points to the guilt of the Talwars.

The judge goes on to speak of the possibility that the Talwars had cleaned the staircase.

> *Possibility of cleaning the blood stains on stairs and railing by the accused after commission of the crime in the night cannot be ruled out as they had enough time and opportunity to do so.*

If the Talwars were indeed the killers the possibility of their cleaning the staircase and railing exists. If the killers were someone else, the possibility of them cleaning the staircase and railing also exists.

So what if there was blood? In what way does this constitute any evidence against the Talwars? A better question to ask here is: How much blood was there? It did not seem to be much. It certainly could have been the blood off the hands or clothes of the killers once they were coming down or going up the stairs, but the killers could have as well been Hemraj's associates or even a third party. The above testimony does seem to indicate that there was 'little' blood, something that the maid Bharti Mandal, who went up the stairs, may not have noticed in a hurry.

The presence or absence of blood on the staircase is clearly a big deal for the judge. There were two bloody murders and one of the dead bodies was found on the terrace. There *would* be blood. The presence of blood alone cannot point to the guilt of the Talwars. No bloodied prints of the Talwars were found on the staircase railing; even the palm print of the killer on the wall of the terrace could not be successfully matched with the palm of either of the Talwars. Dr Rohit Kochhar, a colleague of Rajesh Talwar stated in court that there was a bloodied footprint that appeared to have been wiped off. The police took photographs of a shoeprint off the terrace, but that print was never successfully matched with with those of Rajesh Talwar's own shoes, four pairs of which were seized by the police[39]. That shoe print size was eight or nine but Rajesh Talwar's size was six.[40] Since the shoeprint was never successfully matched with that of anyone else, the only thing that can be said is that there was a man involved for it is unlikely that it was a woman wearing a man's shoes. Until and unless matching shoes were found, that man could have been anyone on the planet.

Going back to the previous point and reading between the lines it appears that the judge wishes to keep open the possibility that Hemraj's artery was severed in Aarushi's room. It is not clear why he wishes to do this; perhaps somewhere he finds it easier to believe that the Talwars were the killers if both throats had been slit in the same place when Rajesh Talwar was under the grips of sudden and violent rage.

But this could not have happened. There is strong evidence that militates against this theory such as the irreversible fact that not a single drop of Hemraj's blood was found in Aarushi's room; even a thorough cleaning up could not have removed DNA presence. The other thing is that had Hemraj's throat been slit in the apartment, while carrying the body upstairs, even if it was placed in a bed sheet, blood would have not only fallen all around but even all the way down to the ground floor. One of the eyewitnesses present at the scene in the immediate aftermath of the killings, a former policeman, Gautam spoke during the course of a television interview about how 'rivers of blood' would have flowed down the staircase.[41] Even had this not been the case, how could the Talwars have been certain that no blood would spill down the stairs and the bed sheet would serve as a catchment area for all the blood? Did they switch on the staircase lights as they carried the corpse or were they stumbling up the staircase under the cover of darkness? Did Nupur Talwar take the front portion of the bed sheet after the husband and wife killer team had tumbled Hemraj's body inside, and Rajesh Talwar the position of the follow up carrier? Presumably the follow up carrier's job is more difficult since the weight is greater? That would also depend on whether the body was being carried head first, or feet first.

Cleaning all the bloody mess up (in the dark or after turning on the staircase lights, which had the potential to wake up neighbours) would have been an impossible nightmare. How they would have trembled when they thought of the possibility of one of the neighbours discovering them hauling a body up the stairs or alternately scrubbing the stairs clean of blood. Even if it is argued that this was an unplanned murder, it would have been a mammoth task to clean blood that may have dripped or fallen all the way to the ground floor. This entire scenario tests the bounds of credibility; and yet this was considered plausible.

The prosecution, defence and the judge himself seem to be struggling against competing possibilities. Elsewhere in the judgement Judge Lal himself concedes that it was possible Hemraj was bludgeoned in the room but his throat was slit later, after his body had been carried to the terrace...

> As he writes: '*It is **also possible** that after bludgeoning Hemraj with golf stick he was carried in a bed sheet by both the accused to the terrace when he was in a state of concussion and thereafter on the terrace his throat was slit and body was dragged*'.[42]

Dead Man's Slippers

The theory that the Talwars killed Hemraj in Aarushi's room and then carried his body upstairs in a bed sheet (bleeding or otherwise) lacks plausibility for yet another reason. Hemraj's dead body was found with slippers on. They could not have been stupid enough to place the slippers onto his feet after he was killed and before carrying him upstairs for the simple reason that slippers have a tendency to fall off.

Were they not worried that Hemraj's slippers would fall off? Or did either Rajesh or Nupur Talwar rush down after his corpse had been left on the terrace, fetch the servant's slippers, insert them on the feet and then presumably wipe their fingerprints off them? One of them did this, but forgot to wipe the blood on the lock to the staircase. They also forgot to wipe the bloodied palm print on the wall. The slippers must have been a priority.

Even if one assumes, that either Rajesh or Nupur somehow wiped their fingerprints off the dead man's slippers, what about their fingerprints over the rest of his body? Another question arises. How does someone wipe their DNA off someone's blood, without getting rid of the blood itself? To be sure the killer/s' DNA and fingerprints would have been all over Hemraj's slippers, body and the bed sheet as well. But those tests and comparisons were never carried out.

Dead Man's Clothes

Hemraj's dead body was found fully clothed on the terrace. This also creates problems with the 'having sex with the girl in the house' theory. The prosecution theory is that Hemraj was having sex with Aarushi when Rajesh Talwar caught them in the act. According to the investigating officer's testimony, Rajesh entered the room with a golf club that he had picked up from Hemraj's room and immediately swung into action. Judge Lal introduces a variation and suggests that Rajesh Talwar rushed off to fetch his golf club and attacked both of them while in this blind, murderous rage. At the time Aarushi would have been unclothed as would have been Hemraj. But Hemraj's dead body was found in the terrace in a fully clothed state.

This opens up two possibilities. Firstly, that Hemraj, caught in the act, was quick enough to jump off the bed and pull on his trousers and shirt, while slow, bumbling Rajesh Talwar went to fetch his murder weapon, the alleged golf club (the judge's view). The alternative scenario is that Hemraj was killed while completely unclothed for Rajesh Talwar entered carrying the golf club with him (as per A.G.L. Kaul, the investigating officer's testimony). In this depiction of events after Hemraj had received blow(s) with the golf club, he unclothed, was then later clothed and carried to the roof.

The point is that if Hemraj were quick enough off the mark to get fully clothed, slippers and all, while Rajesh Talwar went to fetch the golf club, he would also have been alert and agile enough to anticipate and fend off any attack from his master. This would seem to indicate that he was killed unawares while still in a state of undress.

So the prosecution should have fully spelled out step-by-step what exactly happened – remember the Supreme Court decision about each link being established – which it didn't. How easy is it to dress up a naked dead man? How do you put a vest on him and then the shirt and the underwear and trousers? Would Rajesh Talwar have solicited his wife Nupur's help in this regard? The prosecution and the judge did not discuss whether it was possible for Rajesh Talwar to clothe the dead bodies of his daughter and servant alone, or did he need and take the assistance of his wife, Nupur for this too?

That Ringing Phone

If the Talwars were the killers why would they have left Hemraj's phone switched on? And who switched it off after it rang? Records showed that the phone rang somewhere in the NOIDA region and then it was switched off. Was it Rajesh Talwar in the next room who received the call from Nupur who dialled Hemraj's number in the presence of the maid Bharti Mandal? Did Rajesh Talwar then switch off the phone (and later disposed it off)? Was this a pre-planned move? It must have been so, if they were guilty. It shows not only meticulous planning but also great risk taking ability. These days with GPS installed in most phones, with the advancement of technology it is possible to track down the place where a call was received not only in the general location but also within a few yards. As a matter of fact the police did track down that the call was received in the NOIDA area. They could not, however, pinpoint the location to the Talwars' flat, which would surely have cooked their goose had this been technically feasible. How could Rajesh and Nupur Talwar have presumed that the police would not detect that the call was received on a phone that was at the time located within their apartment itself? There have been instances where the police have tracked down a kidnapped child and adult in the boot of a car based on the GPS in the phone. In another case in the UK it was reported in the papers where a man located the dead body of his wife using his wife's phone's GPS.[43] And if that call which Nupur Talwar made to Hemraj had been so tracked and pinpointed – say to Rajesh Talwar's bedroom, their game could have been up, as the evidence would no longer have remained circumstantial. The Talwars displayed such impressive knowledge of communications technology in the country, and the call tracking abilities of investigating agencies; indeed a well planned and such a bold move. There is another thing that remains to be said on this issue. When Nupur called Hemraj on his mobile, according to police records *the phone rang somewhere in NOIDA before it was switched off.*[44] If the phone was in fact with Rajesh Talwar who was in the flat, would not Bharti Mandal, the maid have heard the phone ringing? She would not, of course, have heard the ring if the phone had been put on silent before being switched off. Was Rajesh Talwar then staring at the phone put on silent, and when it rang once, he switched it off? Was this an example of some further coordination on the part of Nupur and Rajesh to fool the maid? This appears difficult to accept. Let us suppose for the sake of argument, that after killing Hemraj, Rajesh Talwar went out and threw the phone somewhere or disposed it off in the dead of night. Could this have happened? The problem with such a theory is that had this been the case, the phone would have either been in a permanenty switched off mode or it would have kept ringing. It would not have rung – and then been switched off!

The Killer's Palm Print

From an investigative point of view, one of the most shocking things about the entire affair is that a bloodied palm print had been left on the terrace wall which could have been easily matched with Rajesh's hand – and if there was a perfect match, or even imperfect, but a match broadly correspondent in terms of overall size and contours – the case against the Talwars would have been immeasurably strengthened. But such was the incompetence of the UP police that something as elementary as this was not done.

It rained some days later and the print was allowed by the investigators to be washed away before a sample could be sent to forensics. The state police and the CBI's second team might have given up too easily it seems for, in an interview the first CBI team's investigating officer stated that despite the rain forensic signs could have still been left on the wall and palm print matching could have been attempted even at that late stage.

If this were indeed possible, a further question arises: why did the second CBI team not attempt to do this? Was it because having cooked the case in terms of circumstantial evidence, they worried that the print would *not* match Rajesh Talwar's palm impression, *effectively ruling him out as the murderer?* It is easy to rule someone out with partial prints of a hand, but on the other hand, it may not be so easy to identify someone with complete certainty. Could it have occurred to the second team that an attempt to match the prints might end up establishing Rajesh Talwar's innocence; at the same time not be a sufficient positive match with the Hemraj's associates or any other suspect to conclusively identify them and convict them as the murderers.

There are other unanswered questions that arise. How does a bloodied handprint on the wall left for the police to match with relevant suspects square with the alleged meticulous planning by the Talwars? On the one hand, you have a 'dressed up' crime scene attributed to the Talwars' meticulous mind-set and on the other, we have this flagrant carelessness – leaving behind a dead give-away bloodied handprint on the wall opposite a murdered victim's dead body. And that was not all. To compound the carelessness the terrace lock (which had to be subsequently broken open) too was stained with blood. Are these the signs of meticulous minds?

The Prosecution Itself Argued That Rajesh Talwar was Innocent

It is worth noting that during the course of the first CBI investigation the state prosecutor himself argued that the Talwars were innocent. On 11 July 2008, after Hemraj's associate Vijay Mandal was arrested, Public Prosecutor R.K. Saini appeared in court to argue for the CBI that Rajesh Talwar should be released. Under the law as it stands if an investigating agency does not find sufficient material or evidence against a suspect who is in custody, it can request the court that he be released.[45]

What Forensic Evidence Remained Could Not Be Successfully Matched

The prosecution did not seek the release of Rajesh Talwar lightly nor would the court have granted it, without concrete basis. The fact of the matter was that there was no direct evidence that could implicate the Talwars.

Although the crime scene had been heavily contaminated, some forensic evidence did remain such as shoeprints, footprints, and the fingerprint on the Ballantine Scotch bottle found on the dining table. If there were a thousand identification marks that could have been compared and matched with the Talwars (and other suspects) nine hundred and fifty were rendered useless because of police incompetence, but fifty such 'markers' still remained. None of the forensic evidence that remained could connect Rajesh Talwar with the crime. The magistrate recorded the following order: 'Vijay Kumar and special prosecutor R.K. Saini mentioned that during the course of the investigation and upon examination of scientific evidence, fingerprints, shoe prints, footprints, clothes, palm prints, etc., the aforesaid evidence could not connect Rajesh Talwar with the crime, therefore his immediate release from custody is sought.'[46] Although the bloodied palm print on the terrace wall was allowed to be washed away, the police did take a photograph of that palm print,[47] which could not, however, be successfully matched with either Rajesh or Nupur, else the prosecution would surely have produced an expert witness to testify on that account. Additionally, Rajesh Talwar's DNA and saliva could not be detected on the whisky bottle, which he was alleged to have been drinking. Since there was no accompanying glass one assumes he would have been drinking from the mouth of the bottle and there would have been some transference of DNA and saliva. None were discovered.[48]

The Activity of the Internet Router on the Night of the Murders

As regards the Internet router, its activity during the course of the night after the murders was used as evidence that the Talwars had committed the murders. It is worth noting, however, that the Internet router showed activity the next day too after the Talwars had left for Haridwar. Among the twenty-six reasons that Judge Shyam Lal listed in his judgement for concluding that the Talwars were guilty, the activity of the Internet router constitutes *two* reasons, so let's discuss the issue in some detail.

Reason six reads as follows:

That the Internet remained active in the night of the gory incident suggesting that at least one of the accused remained awake.

This is clear enough so one cannot take issue with it. However, reason eight also seems connected, which reads as follows:

That there was no disruption in the supply of electricity in that night.

The fact that there was no electricity outage on that fateful night is mentioned as an important ground for establishing that the Talwars were guilty. This was not elaborated upon, although that would have been appropriate.

Listing it as a reason for convicting the Talwars without explaining it further mystified those who read the judgement and were forced to ponder what the judge could possibly have meant by that cryptic statement. One can only conclude what he was saying, which was that the consistent supply of electricity ensured that the computer did not automatically switch off and on.

What was the purpose behind the Talwars' use of the Internet that night, as alleged? The investigators suggested that there could have been information on Aarushi's computer that could have possibly implicated Rajesh and Nupur in the killing. One of the stories that featured in the media was there may have been material related to the Talwars' alleged wife swapping escapades on the machine.

There are several problems with using the Internet router's activity theory as evidence against the Talwars, aside from the fact that it was active even the next day when they were not present in their house. In India telephone and Internet billing is not known to be particularly reliable. Overcharging is not exceptional. People routinely get billed for telephone calls that they have not made; it would therefore surprise no one if this too were the case with Internet activity.

Additionally, the defence team put up formidable arguments against the Internet router's activity leading to the conclusion that the Talwars were awake through much of that fateful night. The cross examination of a Deepak Kanda, nodal officer, Airtel punched holes in the prosecution's arguments, even if these were not accepted by the judge. Kanda, who appeared as prosecution witness number eighteen on behalf of the prosecution, wasn't aware if there was a modem or Wi-Fi at the Talwars' residence as he was never taken to the crime scene. As Judge Lal noted and accepted in his judgement:

> *Deepak Kanda has stated in his cross-examination that he does not know whether there was a modem or a wi-fi; he was never taken to the place where the modem was installed; he does not know that his company had installed the modem along with which a wireless router was also installed; he does not know that if the laptop or desktop computer are switched off then also there will be data transfer between the router/modem and I.S.P. which are switched on; he cannot say whether the log provided to him was a detailed one or not; he has himself admitted that the view of technical team was obtained according to which there were four main reasons for start and stop activity of internet:*
>
> > *(i) physical closing of dialer (ii) physical closing of modem/router (iii) power recycling of modem and (iv) network failures and no member of technical team was examined. Moreover, this witness has also admitted that even from 02:04:35 hours till 10:16:19 hours on 16.05.2008 the usage pattern was similar and start/stop activity was also seen from 02:04:35 hours (in the night) to 13:11:44 hours on 16.05.2008 and thus, physical operation by the accused persons*

> *is not established; he has further argued that P.W.-18* (namely Deepak Kanda) *has also stated in his cross-examination that he never went to L-32, Jalvayu Vihar to make physical inspection; the router, modem, router log or modem log, laptop log or the desktop log were never sent to him; he cannot say whether the logs supplied to him were complete or not; if the router or modem is switched on then log to that extent shall also be available and upon examination of router log it can be said when the router was switched on and switched off and he had written to the investigating officer that computer internet activity log, modem and router log and detailed log of I.S.P. be provided to him but not made available which were essential for complete analysis of these logs and if the investigator had sent the aforesaid details then better analysis could have been done.*

Judge Shyam Lal dismissed the above arguments made by the defence in six crisp words as 'specious and hence cannot be accepted'.

Style and Substance in Judge Shyam Lal's Judgement Style: 'The Cynosure of Judicial Determination'

Let's examine the flowery and archaic linguistic style used by the judge in his judgement the opening paragraph of which reads as follows:

> *The cynosure of judicial determination is the fluctuating fortunes of the dentist couple Dr. Rajesh Talwar and Dr. Nupur Talwar, who have been arraigned for committing and secreting as also deracinating the evidence of commission of the murder of their own adolescent daughter-a beaut damsel and sole heiress Ms. Aarushi and hapless domestic aide Hemraj, who had migrated to India from neighbouring Nepal to eke out living and attended routinely to the chores of domestic drudgery at the house of their masters.*

The mise en scene is Flat No. L-32, Jalvayu Vihar, Sector 25, NOIDA, a suburb of New Delhi. The Dramatis Personae are Dr. Rajesh Talwar, his wife Dr. Nupur Talwar, the accused of this case, Ms. Aarushi and Hemraj, who were bludgeoned and thereafter, jugulated to death on the intervening night of 15/16 May, 2008, Mr. Umesh Sharma and Mrs. Bharti Mandal.

The parties are ad idem that the case is based on circumstantial evidence. Skipping expatiation on prosecution story, a vignette of facts as unveiled is that on 15.05.2008 at about 09:30 P.M. only Dr. Rajesh Talwar, Dr. Nupur Talwar, Ms. Aarushi and Hemraj were last seen in the house by Umesh Sharma, the driver of Dr. Rajesh Talwar and in the morning of 16.05.2008 Ms. Aarushi was found dead in her bedroom, which was adjacent to the bedroom of accused persons and in between these bedrooms there was a ***wooden partition wall****. The dead body of domestic servant Hemraj was found on the terrace of the house on 17.0.2008* ***and there is nothing to suggest that intruder(s) perpetrated this fiendish and flagitious crime****.*

A few comments on this opening paragraph to the judgement are in order. Firstly, this represents a clear departure from the way English is spoken or written nowadays, especially in the Indian subcontinent. The judge has resorted to Victorian English with quaint expressions such as 'daughter-a beaut damsel' and 'sole heiress', the latter expression a throwback to feudal English times when inheritances were especially important. There is also the use of double alliteration, a literary device, such as in 'fluctuating fortunes' 'domestic drudgery' and even 'fiendish and flagitious crime'. Elsewhere in his judgement, Judge Shyam Lal speaks of Hemraj's 'pantaloons' instead of simply the more common and appropriate 'trousers'[49]. In a unique juxtaposition Judge Lal sometimes combines the archaic with modern slang, as he does when he speaks of Hemraj's 'willy' being 'turgid'[50]. Instead of simply stating that Aarushi and Hemraj were having sex, he prefers to say that the two deceased were 'on the job'[51]. In the use of flowery English, Judge Shyam Lal alone cannot be blamed. Many judges in India, including those at the Supreme Court use archaic English to express themselves. Even the redoubtable Krishna Iyer J. of the Supreme Court wrote in one of his classic judgements rendered in *Bangalore Water Supply versus R Rajappa and ors*[52]: 'Legalese and logomacy (sic) have the genius to inject mystique into the meaning of words, thereby alienating the laity from the rule of law.' Apparently he didn't see the contradiction inherent within his words, for he could have made his point in simpler English.

A Wooden Partition Wall, Said the Judge

Although the opening paragraph of Judge Shyam Lal's judgement was reproduced to mainly illustrate the linguistic style he adopts, this does not imply there is nothing to take issue with on the substantive content of this opening paragraph. There is an important factual error here. The judge refers to a 'wooden partition wall'. This reference is important because the prosecution argued that it was highly unlikely that the parents could have slept through an assault and subsequent murder/s in the adjacent room.

On this issue the Talwars defended themselves in two ways. Firstly, they pointed out that the air-conditioner in their room made so much noise that no sounds could penetrate into their room from the outside. Arun Kumar, investigating officer from CBI team one carried out sound tests which indicated that they were speaking the truth. Despite this, the idea that there was a '*wooden* partition wall' affects the value a reader would ascribe to that CBI finding. Although it is technically speaking not inaccurate to say that there was only a wooden partition wall, the fact of the matter is that only a section of it was wooden. Behind the wood, there was solid brick. The wood was there for aesthetic purposes and would have further blocked penetration of the sound, since it was in addition to the brick wall and not a substitute[53].

The judge did make reference to the sound test but did not grant it much weight observing that a '*sound test was carried on 10.06.2008 and it was found that accused sleeping in their bed-room with air-conditioner switched on cannot hear opening and closing/ bolting of entry exit door.*'[54]

That was the least of it. The sound test showed that even shouting and screaming in the next room would not have penetrated the wall because of the sound the air conditioner made. This was not a test carried out by the accused, but a sound test carried out with the help of qualified technicians by the CBI's own leading investigating officer. It was only after this test that DIG Arun Kumar who headed CBI team one was satisfied with the Talwars' story that they didn't hear anything.

Judge Lal discarded the value of the sound test even though it was carried out by the government and investigators and went on to state as follows[55]:

> *Had both the deceased been murdered by an outsider then hearing of the screeches of victims may have certainly awakened the accused persons even if they could be in deep slumber in the adjoining room and the air-conditioner of their room was on* ***as sound travels with more intensity in the night****.*

There are two other important points to be mentioned here. First the fact that Aarushi herself was suffering from laryngitis that may have prevented her from screaming out loud. If there were two assailants one could have covered her mouth while the other assaulted her. Also, the arguments that surely the Talwars would have heard the sound of two bloody murders being carried out in the next room is based on the assumption that there *were* two murders carried out in the room. However, it is equally, if not more likely that Hemraj was killed on the terrace;

and that the action was shifted there precisely because the assailants were worried that the Talwars would wake up.

No Intruders, Said the Judge

There is yet another error in this opening paragraph. It states that there is nothing to suggest there were intruders, which is clearly incorrect. By the expression 'intruders' I understand the judge to mean anyone other than the Talwar family and Hemraj, who entered the apartment without the permission of the Talwars. Hemraj was a teetotaller but empty whisky bottles were found in his room. According to the testimony of Mr Gautam, ex-police officer there was a depression on the bed (suggesting several people may have been sitting on it) and the bathroom was stinking, suggesting use by many people that night (which is likely to have been the case if there were people drinking in the room). The CBI team one had built up a case that the Talwars were innocent and it was the two (or three) intruders that night – Rajkumar, Krishna, and possibly Vijay Mandal who carried out the double murders. So it is rather disingenuous of the judge to say that there was *no suggestion* that there were any intruders that night.

Even if we give the judge's meaning of the word 'outsider' to exclude that trio, there was the tell-tale fingerprint of an outsider on the Ballantine bottle as noted in the CBI Closure Report. That fingerprint did not find a match with either of the Talwars, the associates of Hemraj or anyone else. That there was no evidence of outsiders being present could have been a statement that carried weight if there had been a proper forensic examination and the fingerprints, footprints, DNA etc. of no outsiders were discovered. As things stood the crime scene stood badly contaminated leaving open the possibility that had the crime scene not been disturbed and samples quickly collected with a proper forensic examination carried out, that stranger's fingerprint found on the bottle of Scotch whisky would also have been discovered all over Aarushi's bedroom as well as the terrace.

Substance: Those Twenty-Six Reasons

Discussed earlier was the judge's linguistic style and special vocabulary employed in the opening paragraph, which he cannot, however, sustain for the length of the judgement. Also elaborated and analysed were some points raised in that paragraph.

To now come to the substance, or lack of it, as the case may be. The judge listed as many as twenty-six reasons for convicting the Talwars. If you examine the reasons themselves, you will find that several are simply a narration of facts, others are invalid as 'reasons', and some are imaginary. What can be considered to be 'real' reasons are few and far between. With respect to some reasons adduced, I have offered comments; some reasons are simply ignored such as the first three that cannot be termed as 'reasons' but merely a recital of facts; on others I have decided not to comment because they have been dealt with elsewhere. Here they are, in the judge's own words and the reader may judge for himself:

(1) That irrefragably in the fateful night of 15/16.05.2008 both the accused were last seen with both the deceased in Flat No. L-32, Jalvayu Vihar at about 9.30 P.M. by Umesh Sharma, the driver of Dr. Rajesh Talwar;

(2) That in the morning of 16.05.2008 at about 6.00 A.M. Ms. Aarushi was found murdered in her bed-room which was adjacent to the bedroom of the accused and there was only partition wall between two bed-rooms;

(3) That the dead body of the servant Hemraj was found lying in the pool of blood on the terrace of flat no. L-32, Jalvayu Vihar on 17.05.2008 and the door of terrace was found locked from inside;

(4) That there is a close proximity between the point of time when both the accused and the deceased persons were last seen together alive and the deceased were murdered in the intervening night of 15/16.05.2008 and as such the time is so small that possibility of any other person(s) other than the accused being the authors of the crime becomes impossible;

(5) That the door of Ms. Aarushi's bed-room was fitted with automatic click-shut lock. P.W.-29 Mahesh Kumar Mishra the then S.P. (City), NOIDA has deposed that when he talked to Dr. Rajesh Talwar on 16.05.2008 in the morning, he had told him that in the preceding night at about 11.30 P.M. he had gone to sleep with the key after locking the door of Ms.Aarushi's bed-room from outside. Both the accused have admitted that door of Ms.Aarushi's bed-room was having automatic-click shut lock like that of a hotel, which could not be opened from outside without key but could be opened from inside without key. No explanation has been offered by the accused as to how the lock of Ms. Aarushi's room was opened and by whom;

(6) That the internet remained active in the night of the gory incident suggesting that at least one of the accused remained awake;

(7) That there is nothing to show that an outsider(s) came inside the house in the said night after 9.30 P.M.;

(8) That there was no disruption in the supply of electricity in that night;

(9) That no person was seen loitering near the flats in suspicious circumstances in that night;

(10) That there is no evidence of forcible entry of any outsider(s) in the flat in the night of occurrence;

(11) That there is no evidence of any larcenous act in the flat;

(12) That in the morning of 16th may (sic) 2008 when the maid came to flat for the purpose of cleaning and moping (sic) a false pretext was made by Dr. Nupur Talwar that door might have been locked from outside by the servant Hemraj although it was not locked or latched from outside;

(13) That the house maid Bharti Mandal has nowhere stated that when she came inside the flat both the accused were found weeping;

(14) That from the testimony of Bharti Mandal it is manifestly clear that when she reached the flat and talked to Dr. Nupur Talwar then at that time she had not complained about the murder of her daughter and rather she told the maid deliberately that Hemraj might have gone to fetch milk from Mother Dairy after locking the wooden door from outside. This lack of spontaneity is relevant under Section 8 of the Evidence Act;

(15) That the clothes of both the accused were not found soaked with the blood. It is highly unnatural that parents of deceased Ms. Aarushi will not cling to and hug her on seeing her murdered;

(16) That no outsider(s) will dare to take Hemraj to the terrace in severely injured condition and thereafter search out a lock to be placed in the door of the terrace;

(17) That it is not possible that an outsider(s) after committing the murders will muster courage to take Scotch whisky knowing that the parents of the deceased Ms. Aarushi are in the nearby room and his top priority will be to run away from the crime scene immediately; ***Comment:*** *The presence of a bottle of Ballantine does not implicate the Talwars at all. It was the easiest thing in the world for them to have got rid of it. Moreover they were fingerprints on the bottle that did not match the Talwars. How could the Talwars have transplanted the fingerprints of a stranger on to the bottle?*

(18) That no outsider(s) will bother to take the body of Hemraj to the terrace. Moreover, a single person cannot take the body to the terrace; ***Comment:*** *Even if the judge is right in saying that a single person could not have carried Hemraj's body to the terrace, how does that in any way implicate the Talwars? Could there not have been two or more outsiders? CBI Team One suspected Rajkumar, Krishna and Vijay Mandal. Could they not have carried the body to the terrace? Is it also not possible that Hemraj went upstairs voluntarily with Rajkumar and Krishna or with some other outsider and was murdered at that location?*

(19) That the door of the terrace was never locked prior to the occurrence but it was found locked in the morning of 16.05.2008 and the accused did not give the key of the lock to the police despite being asked to give the same;

(20) That the accused have taken plea in the statements under Section 313 Cr.P.C. that about 8-10 days before the occurrence painting of cluster had started and the navvies used to take water from water tank placed on the terrace of the flat and then Hemraj had started locking the door of the terrace and the key of that lock remained with him. If it was so then it was not easily possible for an outsider to find that key.

Comment: *Isn't it also possible that Hemraj himself walked up the stairs leading to the terrace and opened the door himself not suspecting that he would be killed?*

(21) That if an outsider(s) may have committed the crime in question after locking the door of terrace and had gone out of the flat then the outer most mesh door or middle mesh door must have been found latched from outside;

(22) That the motive of commission of the crime has been established;

(23) That it is not possible that after commission of the crime an outsider(s) will dress-up the crime scene;

(24) That golf-club no. 5 was thrown in the loft after commission of the crime and the same was produced after many months by the accused Dr. Rajesh Talwar;

Comment: *This is an improper presentation of the facts. The thought that a golf club may have been the murder weapon occurred to CBI Team Two very late in the day " a year and a half later. If he had wished, Rajesh Talwar had ample time to destroy that piece of evidence. In fact, Rajesh Talwar himself handed over the golf club to CBI Team Two, which was presented as the murder weapon.*

(25) That pattern of head and neck injuries of both the accused persons are almost similar in nature and can be caused by golf-club and scalpel respectively;

(26) That the accused Dr. Rajesh Talwar was a member of the Golf-Club, NOIDA and golf clubs were produced by him before the C.B.I. and scalpel is used by the dentists and both the accused are dentists by profession;

Comment: Would not the Talwars have realised that if the injuries were very precise and surgical (as was alleged) it would direct the needle of suspicion towards them? Moreover, a team from AIIMS concluded that the injuries could have been inflicted by a khukri. *Why would they use a scalpel in preference to a kitchen knife?*

The Supreme Court on Circumstantial Evidence and Convictions

A recent Supreme Court judgement on the question of convictions based solely on circumstantial evidence is relevant to the Aarushi case. Judge Shyam Lal quotes the ratio or essential part of the ruling, but had not, in my view, applied it to the facts of the Aarushi case. In *Sathya*

Narayan versus State[56] five golden principles are outlined and referred to as follows[57]:

> (1) *The circumstances from which the conclusion of guilt is to be drawn should be fully established. The circumstances must be or should and not may be established;*
>
> (2) *The facts so established should be consistent only with the hypothesis of the guilt of the accused, that is to say, they should not be explained on any other hypothesis except that the accused is guilty;*
>
> (3) *The circumstances should be of a conclusive nature and tendency;*
>
> (4) *They should exclude every possible hypothesis except the one to be proved;*
>
> (5) *There must be a chain of evidence so complete as not to leave any reasonable ground for the conclusion consistent with the innocence of the accused and must show that in all human probability the act must have been done by the accused.*
>
> *These five golden principles constitute the **'Panch Sheel'** of the proof of a case based on circumstantial evidence.'*

Let us consider if these five principles were complied within the context of the Aarushi case for only then could the conviction been sustained as per the law laid down by the highest court in the land.

The first principle:

*The circumstances from which the conclusion of guilt is to be drawn should be **fully** established.*

Are the circumstances of the two killings 'fully' established? By no means.

The second principle:

The facts so established should be consistent only with the hypothesis of the guilt of the accused, that is to say, they should not be explained on any other hypothesis....

This golden principle also stands violated. In fact there *was* another hypothesis that the investigative agency (CBI Team One) considered to be *more* credible for a considerable length of time. This was the view that it was the associates of Hemraj who had committed the murders. The Aarushi case was not a case where there was no other credible hypothesis.

The second principle has an overlap with the fourth principle, which requires:

> *They (the circumstances) should exclude every possible hypothesis except the one to be proved.*

In part three of this book I venture to suggest yet another possibility. There may not be any evidence to suggest that this happened, but it is possible that someone known to Aarushi, other than the associates of Hemraj was the killer. Fingerprints discovered on the Ballantine bottle did not match with either the Talwars or any of the other suspects suggesting there was some other person (CBI closure report). This fingerprint of an unknown person on a bottle with bloodstains was never explained. Was that same fingerprint found elsewhere in the apartment or on the terrace? We will never know because the crime scene was so heavily contaminated and in any case no investigation was done on this basis.

The fifth principle speaks of the need for the chain of evidence to be so complete so as not to leave any reasonable possibility that the accused were innocent.

Was the chain of evidence complete? Judge Shyam Lal is not even certain where Hemraj's artery was severed. It could have been Aarushi's bedroom or it could have been done on the terrace. He concedes that 'it could *also* have been possible' that Hemraj's throat was slit after taking his body to the terrace. That link in the chain of evidence is completely broken, hanging somewhere between the terrace and the bedroom of the Talwar residence and is by no means 'complete'.

Let us hear from the Supreme Court in another decision on the 'chain of evidence.' In *Dharam Das Wadhwani versus State of U.P.*[58], it was held by the apex court that 'every evidentiary circumstance is a probative link, strong, or weak, and must be made out with certainty. Link after link, forged firmly by credible testimony may form a strong chain of sure guilt binding the accused'.

Illustrations of Faulty Reasoning in the Aarushi Case

The mismatch continues. On a first reading of Judge Shyam Lal's judgement on several pages I experienced complete bafflement and consternation. It took me a second reading to understand why this was the case. Judge Lal was quoting Supreme Court justices and international jurists extensively, so no one could accuse him of not having read the law. But he wasn't applying that very same law in its true meaning. He could not, however, have accomplished his final result of convicting both the Talwars without, in my view, serious distortions and misappraisal of the evidence. Faulty reasoning resonates through several parts of the judgement. A sample follows:

On Hemraj, the teetotaller

On page sixty-nine the judge observes:

> *There is no evidence of egress and ingress; there is no evidence of any larcenous act; there is no evidence of any forcible entry inside the flat; there is no evidence at all to suggest that friends of Hemraj came inside the flat after 9.30 P.M. and shared drinks of liquor with Hemraj. In the post-mortem examination report of Hemraj no finding has been given that liquor contents were found in his stomach and no suggestion has been given before any witness that Hemraj had taken alcohol with his friends in that night. It is well-nigh impossible that Hemraj will dare to booze with his friends in his servant room particularly when the accused persons were very much present in the nearby room.*

Comment: The judge remarks:

(T)here is no evidence at all to suggest that friends of Hemraj came inside the flat after 9.30 P.M. and shared drinks of liquor with Hemraj.

The above remarks would seem to suggest that the defence had suggested that Hemraj himself had consumed alcohol on the night of the murders. The defence made no such averment and consistently maintained that it was Hemraj's friends or associates who were drinking that night. The Talwars too always maintained that their servant Hemraj was a teetotaller.

They why should the judge bring up the issue of no liquor having been discovered in Hemraj's stomach during the course of the post-mortem, creating an illusion in the mind of an uninformed reader that the judge was actually making some deductions here. I consider this to be the faulty reasoning of a judge who has already made up his mind.

The Question of Reasonable Doubt and Shifting Burden of Proof

American Judge Chief Justice Shaw in his decision in the famous Webster case explains the concept of 'reasonable doubt' in eloquent terms[59]:

'It is not mere possible doubt, because everything relating to human affairs and depending upon moral evidence is open to some possible or imaginary doubt. It is that state of the case which, after the entire comparison and consideration of all the evidence, leaves the minds of the jurors in that consideration that they cannot say they feel an abiding conviction to a moral certainty of the truth of the charge'.

An abiding conviction to a moral certainty of the truth of the charge....

It is true as Judge Shyam Lal observed that it is nearly impossible in any criminal trial to prove all the elements with a scientific precision. Chief Justice Fletcher Moulton remarked that 'proof does not mean rigid mathematical formulae since that is impossible'.[60] However, this does not mean that accused persons can be convicted without sufficient proof, as happened in the case of the Talwars.

What makes matters worse is that in some respects Judge Shyam Lal expected the Talwars to prove their innocence! I believe he has misinterpreted the law in this regard. Judge Lal appears to have been influenced by a decision that relates to the shifting of the burden of proof. I quote from his judgement[61]:

> He quotes from a pre-Independence decision, *Radhey Lal and others Vs. Emperor*[62] pointing out that '*it was held by the Hon'ble Justice Allsop that an accused person is required to explain the circumstances which appear against him in the evidence and if he cannot or will not do so, he must take the consequences. If he chooses to take up the position that he relies upon the technicality that the whole burden of proof was upon the prosecution and refuses to say anything about the matter, he can hardly be surprised if he is convicted upon the evidence produced by the prosecution, if that proves circumstances from which his guilt can be inferred.*

The judge then goes on to refer to Section 106 of the Evidence Act, which provides that '*when any fact is especially within the knowledge of any person, the burden of proving that fact is upon him*'.

By making the above references and observations Judge Shyam Lal appears to argue that the burden of proof had shifted to the Talwars. They needed to prove, in his view, that if they were not the killers, who *were* the killers? There may be cases where the burden of proof shifts to the accused as in the case of a death in police custody, but the logic of that custodial situation did not apply in the Aarushi murder case. There may be some other cases or situations where it can shift but this was not such a case.

Let me illustrate this further.

An accused person dies in the police lock up with severe wounds all over his body. Policemen in charge of that lock-up can be required to explain how the prisoner died, because this is a case where they have special knowledge of the circumstances. The same goes for custodial rape.

Or consider a more interesting and contemporary example. A celebrity filmstar and his driver are the occupants of a car that killed several pedestrians in an accident. If he, the actor, states in court that he himself was not at the wheel, he has to then also state who *was* at the wheel. He has special knowledge of the circumstances and he cannot simply insist that it is up to the prosecution to prove who was driving the car when the accident occurred. This is because he cannot credibly state that he did not know who was driving or did not see who was driving.

The Aarushi case is not comparable and the context is completely different. The Talwars could not be expected to know who the assailants were, since they themselves were sleeping, according to their own account and testimony. They could not have been expected to provide independent verification that they were indeed sleeping. It was nighttime and they would have gone to sleep in the normal course of events. 'Special knowledge' may only be attributed to them only if the prosecution had been able to prove beyond all reasonable doubt that the duo were not sleeping or even if asleep could not have remained asleep. The onus was not on the Talwars to prove that they fell asleep and remained asleep. In the absence of such proof, how on earth could they be expected to know, who, if not they, were the killers? At first Rajesh Talwar thought he did know; he was in fact convinced that Hemraj had murdered his daughter. Later when Hemraj's dead body was discovered, he realised he had got it all wrong. If he got it wrong once, he could get it wrong again. He could not then in all fairness insist with any degree of confidence that it was Krishna, the compounder or Rajkumar or indeed anyone else. For not suggesting any more that a particular person was the killer, he and his wife, Nupur do not deserve to be penalised in any way.

That Judge Lal completely misunderstood the concept of shifting 'burden of proof' as applicable in the Aarushi case is further evident from the following observations he makes in his judgement[63]:

> ***(I)t was incumbent upon the accused to establish as to how the body of Hemraj was taken to the roof by whom and who had locked the terrace door from inside (sic) but they have miserably failed to establish the same.*** *It is not expected of the prosecution to lead evidence on the point which is exclusively within the knowledge and domain of the accused. Thus, the argument of the learned counsel is devoid of any merit....*

So, the Talwars who were busy sleeping are somehow supposed to have exclusive knowledge even in their state of slumber of what is happening outside their bedroom. The judge argues that 'it is not expected of the prosecution to lead evidence on the point which is exclusively within the knowledge and domain of the accused'. Further, 'it was incumbent upon the accused to establish as to how the body of Hemraj was taken to the roof'. Not only this, but they have to substitute the investigators (who confessed in the Closure Report that they could not be certain who the killers were) and tell the court that if it wasn't them then who was the hell it was.

On the Establishment of a Motive

On the issue of motive, at one point in the judgement Judge Lal states that the motive is proved and in fact lists it as one of the twenty-six reasons why he found the Talwars guilty of the killings. This is reason number twenty-two and instead of elaborating on what the motive really was there is only a single line which reads as follows:

> *That the motive of commission of the crime has been established.*

Elsewhere in the judgement, however, as if he has bitten off more than he can chew he says that it is not necessary to establish motive. It appears that the judge is not really sure whether motive has been proved. Why else would he quote the Supreme Court in the case of *State of Karnataka verus David Rosario* to the effect that 'where credible evidence exists on record to establish guilt of the accused, it is not necessary to find out the motive of the crime'. To reiterate that Judge Shyam Lal is unsure of himself on the question of establishment of motive for the crime this is what he has to say in another part of the judgement: '*It is a matter of common knowledge that many murders have been committed without any known or prominent motive.* ***Mere fact that prosecution has failed to translate that mental disposition of the accused into evidence does not mean that no such mental condition existed in the mind of the assailant***'.

It seems as if the judge is saying the motive was established, but even if it was not established it does not matter. Heads I win, and tails, you still lose. The other thing is how can the judge be so sure that the motive is established because A.G.L. Kaul, the investigator has himself acknowledged in the Closure Report submitted by him on behalf of the CBI that one important reason advanced for seeking closure and non-prosecution of anyone was the fact that it had been unable to establish motive.

On the Tutored Evidence of the Maid

On page eighty-seven the judge observes as follows:

> *Mr. Mir has criticized the evidence of Mrs. Bharti Mandal on the fulcrum that she was thoroughly tutored before stepping into the witness box and she has admitted this*

fact in her cross-examination and therefore, no reliance can be placed upon her testimony.

The evidence of the maid, Bharti Mandal was of great importance because she was the first person in the morning to enter the premises and witness the reaction and behaviour of the Talwars; and also because her evidence in court was interpreted by the prosecution to mean that the door of the Talwar residence could have been closed from inside.

Before we get into her actual testimony it is necessary to provide some background that will make its significance clear to the reader. There were three doors to the Talwar residence. Starting from the inside there was first a wooden door and then just besides it a mesh door. There is then the passage, which led up to a third, final door that was a grilled door. One had the possibility of entering the passage through either the mesh door or through a door that led to Hemraj's room.

Normally one can expect that the maid will ring the bell, stand outside the grill door and wait for someone to open the door from inside. On that morning Bharti Mandal, who was temporarily filling in for the Talwars' regular maid did just that. She rang the bell and waited. What happened in the few minutes after she rang the bell and she was finally let in is of crucial importance.

Nupur Talwar opened the wooden door. Bharti and Nupur saw each other through the mesh door. Nupur found that she could not get past the mesh door to let Bharti in, and assumed that it had been locked from outside by Hemraj who Nupur assumed had gone to fetch milk from Mother Diary[64]. So she told Bharti just this that Hemraj had gone and would be soon returning and she should just wait outside for him to return.

Bharti Mandal was a busy woman, and besides she was working for the Talwars on a temporary basis, so she did not like the idea of simply waiting. She reminded Nupur that there was a duplicate key for the mesh door and suggested that she, Bharti, would go down and Nupur could down the key to her from the balcony, to which suggestion Nupur agreed.[65]

Bharti Mandal went down to collect the key, and saw Nupur appear on the balcony. **Nupur now told Bharti that the mesh door had not been locked from outside but had merely been bolted[66].** How could Nupur have known this? She could have possibly looked from the side just as Bharti went down and seen that it was bolted. Or perhaps she shook the door slightly and from its movement realised that the door was bolted and not locked. These small details are unfortunately not available in the testimony of the witnesses.

Bharti suggested that Nupur throw down the 'long key' anyhow, which Nupur did. And then Bharti climbed up the stairs once again, pushed open the grill door, saw that the mesh door was bolted, unbolted it and entered the apartment. She said as much in her testimony[67].

'Then I unbolted the mesh door...'

Did the fact that the mesh door was bolted from outside provide conclusive evidence that the Talwars were innocent? Not really, because assuming that they were the killers they could have accessed the passage through Hemraj's door, bolted the door and re-entered the apartment through Hemraj's door.

Far greater significance lies in the words Bharti uttered in her testimony to the courts *before* she uttered that part about unbolting the mesh door.

She stated in court as follows:

'I touched the iron (outermost grill) door but it did not open...'[68]

Now this was a statement that Bharti had not made to any of the previous investigators who had interviewed her. One possible implication of her statement which the prosecution drew upon, was that that grill door did not open because it was locked from inside!

If indeed the grill door was locked from inside, it would be clear that the Talwars *were* the killers.

The prosecution suggested to the court that the grill door was locked from inside. In their view of the matter, following Bharti Mandal's arrival in the morning, Nupur Talwar quickly realised that this would implicate them and therefore sent Bharti downstairs. As soon as Bharti went down, Nupur rushed to Hemraj's room, pushed aside the fridge blocking the door to the passage, opened the door, entered the passage, unlocked the grill door, bolted the mesh door, went back into Hemraj's room, pushed the fridge back in place, rushed to fetch the key to the mesh door and then went to the balcony to see Bharti waiting for her. That Nupur could have been so galvanised into a flurry of activity, tasks that an athelete would be hard put to accomplish in the course of a couple of minutes, seems unlikely but this is the idea that the prosecution threw out, which appealed enormously to Judge Shyam Lal.

The question the prosecution posed was this: Since Bharti Mandal stated: 'I *touched* the iron door but it did not open,' surely this meant that the door was bolted from inside?

Not necessarily.

Four things can be said in defence of the Talwars in this regard.

Firstly, the idea that Nupur Talwar could have accomplished all these tasks within a few minutes seems implausible. What would happen if the maid suddenly came back up to see her in the passage bolting the mesh door? The game would be up. Could Nupur have taken that risk?

Secondly, there was the testimony of witnesses to the effect that the outer grill door had a tendency to jam.

Shashi Devi, a washerwoman who ironed clothes for the Talwars made a statement to Hari Singh, one of the investigators that that particular door was always open but it jammed frequently and she would need to push really hard to get it open, and then once it was open she would just leave the clothes in the passage[69]. Judge Shyam Lal points out in his judgement that this person did not appear as a witness in his court[70]. However, Hari Singh did give evidence in this regard, confirming that the washerwoman had made that statement[71]. There was also the driver of the Talwars, Umesh who made a statement to the effect that the outermost door could be opened by pushing it hard[72]. However, Judge Shyam Lal dismissed his testimony using the unusual epithet 'traitor' to describe him.

Thirdly, all Bharti Mandal said was that she 'touched' the iron door but it did not open. She did not say that she pushed the door, and that it still did not open. Grill doors are usually heavy being made of iron and unless they are well oiled do not open upon a mere touch.

And finally, Bharti Mandal had never made this statement on any previous occasion about 'touching' the grill door, which did not open. There was therefore the possibility that the prosecution had prevailed upon her to make this statement in order to buttress an extremely weak case.

The Talwars' lawyer did not let them down at this juncture.

During cross-examination, he managed to get Bharti Mandal to confess that she had been tutored.

> '*I am only speaking as I had been instructed to,*' were Bharti's exact words, reported widely in the media. In the original Hindi it was '*Mujhe jaisa samjhaya gaya hai, wahi bayan main yahan dey rahi hoon.*'[73]

Witnesses, said Jeremy Bentham, the famous English philosopher and jurist, are the eyes and ears of justice. If a witness confesses to having been tutored, it destroys or at least significantly lowers the credibility of that witness.

Judge Shyam Lal is shockingly overindulgent here, just as he was with respect to the testimony of the doctors that appeared on behalf of the prosecution. In a departure from established rules for assessing the credibility of a witness's testimony, he reasons as follows:

> *One must not forget that P.W.-10 Bharti Mandal* ***is totally illiterate and bucolic lady from a lower-strata of the society*** *and hails from Malda District of West Bengal who came to NOIDA to perform menial job to sustain herself and family and* therefore, *if she has stated that she has given her statement on the basis of tutoring, her evidence cannot be discarded or rejected.*[74]

On the issue that Bharti's testimony was not consistent with her earlier statements, Judge Lal goes on to merrily add another 'merely' as follows[75]

> *Merely because there is inconsistency in evidence, it is not sufficient to impair the credit of the witness.*

Bharti Mandal was smart enough not to accept Nupur's suggestion that she wait for Hemraj and requested her to throw down the key. She is described as 'totally illiterate and bucolic', which form the apparent basis for the judge to react indulgently to the tutoring she has received. Many illiterate people are as, or more, intelligent than the average educated person. We have a population in which millions of people continue to remain illiterate – should the police be permitted to coach and tutor them in serious criminal cases, and should the judges tolerate such tutoring?

There are some instances where an element of tutoring can be permissible such as in the case of a very young child. Even in the case of a young child's testimony, where tutoring may not invalidate the entire testimony, our Supreme Court has held that an attempt should be made to separate the tutored segment from the untutored segment before placing any reliance on the testimony[76]. Bharti Mandal was no child.

Judge Lal seems to be creating a new kind of jurisprudence here, on his own, for he does not cite the opinion of any higher judicial authorities that endorse the position he has taken with respect to the tutoring of witnesses. Bharti is described as 'lower strata' with the suggestion thrown in that she cannot have the confidence to depose in court, and needs tutoring.

Bharti Mandal is also described as 'bucolic', which is not a mental defect or related in any way to being an alcoholic but simply means someone hailing from the countryside. So should the millions of our countrymen residing in the villages have a different law of evidence framed for them – one that would be more accepting of tutoring by the police and investigators? Consider how such a policy would impact the rights of accused persons, especially in trials involving serious offences, where a verdict can potentially be a matter of life or death.

The Verdict and the Sentence

Judge Lal clearly devoted special attention, in the manner of an erstwhile student of literature to the crafting of his opening and concluding paragraphs. Quoting the injunctions against the taking of human life from three prominent religions in the country, towards the end of his judgement, he writes as follows:

> *Now is the time to say omega in this case. To perorate, it is proved beyond reasonable doubt that the accused are the perpetrators of the crime in question. The parents are the best protectors of their own children " that is the order of human nature but there have been freaks in the history of mankind when the father and mother became the killer of their own progeny. They have extirpated their own daughter who had hardly seen 14 summers of her life and the servant without compunction from terrestrial terrain in breach of*

*Commandment '**Thou shall not kill'** and injunction of Holy Quran – '**Take not life, which God has made sacred'.** They are also found guilty of secreting and obliterating the evidence of the commission of the murders to screen themselves from legal punishment. In addition to that Dr. Rajesh Talwar is also found guilty of furnishing false information to the police regarding the murder of his daughter by Hemraj. Dharmo Rakshati Rakshat i.e. if we protect "Dharma", Dharma will protect us. If we protect "Law", law will protect us.*

Having found the Talwars guilty Judge Shyam Lal awarded them the maximum possible sentence. Theoretically, as per the law laid down by the Supreme Court, for the crime of murder, it would have been possible for him to sentence the two to death if the case came within the compass of the 'rarest of rare' cases involving some particular brutality, depravity and the like. The judge considered the possibility but realised and ruled that the case clearly did not fall within that category.

Judge Lal convicted both husband and wife of murder (under Section 302 Indian Penal Code) and sentenced them to rigorous imprisonment for life. That was not all. He also found the Talwars guilty of causing the disappearance of evidence (under Section 201 Indian Penal Code) and for this crime sentenced them to an additional five years of rigorous imprisonment. A few words may be said about this additional crime the Talwars are said to have committed.

Causing the Disappearance of Evidence

Section 201 of the Indian Penal Code constitutes the crime causing the disappearance of evidence relating to an offence. Disappearance, in some instances may also mean the destruction of evidence. Section 203 of the Indian Penal Code provides that giving out false information in respect of an offence is itself a crime.

The Talwars were found guilty by Judge Lal of wilfully causing evidence to disappear, and five years rigorous imprisonment was added to the life sentence imposed on them for the murders. This seems disingenuous if we consider how much evidence was there on the crime scene and how the state police allowed the evidence/crime scene to get contaminated. Perhaps the inability to conserve evidence by the police (which has ipso facto the same results as 'destruction' of evidence) also needs to be made an offence, even if on a lesser scale, to force the police to hone up their investigative skills?

It is ironical that the Talwars were accused of causing evidence to disappear. All the evidence was there, starting at the investigators. Rather, it was the police that permitted the crime scene to be contaminated and compromised.

Even the alleged murder weapon, the golf club, was handed over by Rajesh Talwar himself to the police; the police could not even discover this by themselves. And then the prosecution accused Rajesh Talwar of causing evidence to disappear and 'hiding' that weapon.

Just a Little Extra Punishment for Dr Rajesh Talwar

The prime driver of the murders, according to the prosecution, was Dr Rajesh Talwar, and Nupur, his wife, was his active and loyal collaborator. They received an identical punishment for the crime of murder and causing the disappearance of evidence. This may have seemed just a bit imbalanced to Saza Lal as Judge Shyam Lal was commonly referred to in the Ghaziabad courts given his penchant for convicting rather than acquitting. Even judges inclined to punish have a sense of equity. And therefore Rajesh Talwar was convicted for another offence " that of furnishing false information and sentenced to an additional one year of simple imprisonment. The judge does not, however, explain anywhere how he came to the conclusion that it was only Rajesh and Nupur who provided false information.

Not Even a Small Spanking for the Police

The judge did not find it fit to pass any strictures against the police for the bungled investigation; rather at various places in his judgement, which I have previously referred to, he seeks to condone and overlook their mistakes (and those of the doctors who appear for the prosecution). If this is a senior judge how will the police and investigators become top-notch? Other Aarushis will be waiting to happen, where similar bungling may occur, leaving wide open the possibility of innocents languishing in prisons for years on end.

On Judges who are Pre-Disposed to Convict

The lawyers at the Ghaziabad courts advised the counsel representing the Talwars to somehow delay the matter such that Judge Shyam Lal would retire before he had a chance to pronounce a verdict in the Aarushi case[77]. In criminal courts across the world, there exist judges that are more inclined to convict than to acquit. A judge with a pre-disposition to convict is feared by lawyers and accused persons alike. While accused persons are not happy to be tried by judges that convict all too frequently, the relatives of victims of violent crimes will be distressed by verdicts that seem to acquit all too easily. Judges have 'tendencies' just like the rest of the population does, and our ideal notion of a judge is at variance from the reality not only in India but across the world.

I cannot of course speak for the rest of the world, but in the Indian context I am aware of certain factors that play subconsciously or consciously in the minds of judges that are more inclined to convict. If a judge presiding over a criminal trial lets off an accused person for lack of evidence, he can worry that his colleagues, especially his detractors, would shrug their shoulders contemptuously and gossip that he had been purchased. At some conscious or subconscious level Judge Lal may have been aware that if he convicted the Talwars, the public baying for the blood of the killers would be satiated and furthermore no one could then accuse him of taking a pay off. This might seem to be perverted reasoning and perhaps it is, but one has to understand that a corrupt judicial environment can affect judges. When a judge decides to acquit someone, he may have done so because of insufficient evidence, but if the accused was high profile word may get around that the judge took money. On the other hand in the case of a conviction he won't be accused of this allegation unless there were special circumstances, viz a powerful business or political rival was seeking to have a man convicted.

So, if one wants to gain a reputation for honesty and integrity within the legal fraternity, as a judge in trial courts in India, you probably need to slowly tilt towards convictions. The other thing is that the state of investigation is frequently so poor that judges sometimes feel compelled to issue their own corrective and issue convictions even when the prosecution's case has not been sufficiently buttressed by credible evidence. Say, when a judge is hearing a case involving a professional criminal, even if there is insufficient evidence 'beyond all reasonable doubt' he may apply his own corrective and lower that threshold. There is no legal justification to do so, but he may, in his own subjective world-view feel morally impelled to do so when it is a case of a particularly gruesome murder or rape.

This is not to in any way suggest that Judge Lal succumbed to any of these pressures, but merely to point out that they exist.

In Conclusion

Following the release of the film *Talvar* and the fresh controversy it generated, Arun Kumar, investigating officer of CBI Team One was interviewed. The officer stated that he continued to believe in the innocence of the Talwars. Few people would be more familiar with the facts of the case than Arun Kumar. As a matter of fact, he was closer in terms of time to the events than A.G.L. Kaul the officer who eventually replaced him.

Arun Kumar is not your run-of-the-mill crime investigator; he has investigated high profile crimes in the country such as the Telgi scam, a case involving an eventually convicted Indian counterfeiter who may have sold bogus Indian stamps worth Rs 20,000 crores.[78] He is therefore not a man that is fooled easily. There are many reasons why he believed the Talwars to be innocent. One of the factors that influenced him, he stated in his interview, was that he believed it was impossible for the Talwars to be certain that the door to the terrace would not be opened and Hemraj's dead body discovered there. 'Forensic samples were never collected,' he laments, referring to the botched up investigation by the state police before the CBI took over the case. 'If they had been, the case could have been solved very easily.'[79]

I would argue that for various reasons that have been advanced (too numerous to list even briefly, once again) the Talwars should have been acquitted.

Many would even say this is roulette-wheel justice; not true justice. The court should have considered that a theory could be built around a certain set of facts to indict anyone. If the investigation, and the investigators themselves (CBI Team One and CBI Team Two) stand more or less equipoised between two alternative scenarios " prosecuting the Talwars on the one hand, and prosecuting Hemraj's associates on the other hand, *ipso facto* this is not a case that can be proved against either group beyond the legal threshold of reasonable doubt.

To use an analogy many readers will be familiar with i.e. the language of cricket. The pitch can be considered to constitute the territory of 'reasonable doubt'. When Judge Shyam Lal spelled out his twenty-six reasons for holding the Talwars guilty of double murder, perhaps he used the analogy in his mind of a batsman hitting a cricket ball, which rises higher and higher with each additional reason advanced, finally clearing the boundary. In my considered view, it was not a sixer that our judicial batsman hit; despite his determined and bold stroke a player caught the ball at the mid-field well before reaching the boundary.

Part - Two

The Servant's Associates Committed the Two Murders

Rather let the crime of the guilty go unpunished, than condemn the innocent
Justinian 1, *Law Code*, AD 535

List of Characters

The Suspects (who were all released, with Aarushi's parents being charged instead)

1. Krishna Thadarai, the Talwars' compounder
2. Rajkumar Sharma, who worked in the house of the Durranis, both dentists who were friends and worked with the Talwars
3. Vijay Mandal, who worked for Puneesh Tandon, a neighbour

The Victims

4. Aarushi Talwar, a fourteen year old teenager, the Talwars' only daughter
5. Hemraj, the family servant

The Investigating Officers

6. Team One – the NOIDA police
7. Team Two – the first CBI team, which took over fifteen days after the killings, headed by Deputy Inspector General Arun Kumar

8. Team Three – the second CBI team headed by Additional Superintendent of Police A.G.L. Kaul

The Judge

9. Judge Shyam Lal, additional sessions and district judge, Ghaziabad

THE SERVANT'S ASSOCIATES COMMITTED THE TWO MURDERS

An Alternative Scenario and Sequence of Events

In the previous section we used the CBI Team Two's investigating officer's statement in court to reconstruct the alleged sequence of events, based on the clear proposition that the Talwars were the killers.

Had the CBI team not been switched it is probable that Team One, the original CBI team would have charged Krishna and Rajkumar, the associates of Hemraj with the murders. Vijay Mandal, the third associate may have been charged with lesser offences if at all there was a plan to make him an approver. An approver is someone who is involved in a crime but agrees to confess and implicate co-accused in exchange for receiving a pardon.

The following sequence of events is based on the hypothesis that the associates of the servant Hemraj killed both Aarushi and Hemraj.[80]

1. Two of Hemraj's associates were drinking in Hemraj's room. This was Rajkumar, the Durranis' servant, and Krishna, the compounder. They were drinking beer and Sula wine. The alcohol finished, and the two associates prevailed on Hemraj to get some liquor from Dr Rajesh Talwar's liquor cabinet. In their drunken state both Krishna and Rajkumar start passing lewd comments about Aarushi, much to Hemraj's disapproval. As Hemraj went off to get some whisky from Rajesh Talwar's cabinet, Krishna and Rajkumar quickly entered Aarushi's room, the

door to which was open. (Incidentally, A.G.L. Kaul the CBI Team Two's investigating officer deposed that in his view the door to Aarushi's room was open; however, Judge Shyam Lal believed that the door was closed and writes as much in his judgement). Krishna and Rajkumar shut the door behind them and the self-locking mechanism swung into place which meant that no one else could now have entered the room, unless it was opened from inside or he possessed the keys.

2. Aarushi woke up immediately after hearing the two enter and switched on the light. From the expression on Rajkumar and Krishna's faces she understood their intentions at once and tried to shout for help, but one of the assailants covered her mouth. She continued to struggle and in the process some of her toys and other things were disturbed. Eventually though she was overpowered.
3. Rajkumar and Krishna force her down and onto the bed. One of them keeps Aarushi's mouth covered with his hand. The other threatens her with the *khukri*, which they brought into the room to frighten her. She is terrified at seeing the knife and stops struggling. Meanwhile one of the two assailants removes her pyjamas with a view to sexually violate her. Aarushi tries to scream but her mouth is covered and no sound escapes her; she also happens to be suffering from laryngitis.
4. Meanwhile, Aarushi opens her mouth once more to scream. Before she can utter a second sound, in a sudden panic that her shouts will awaken the Talwars, one of the assailants hits her with the flat end of the khukri. She immediately falls unconscious, and is half dead.
5. Meanwhile, Hemraj the servant had fetched a bottle of Ballantine from Rajesh Talwar's cabinet and placed it on top of the dining table. He starts to wonder where his friends are, when the noises

coming from Aarushi's room make him realise that they are in Aarushi's room with less than honourable intentions. He keeps knocking and whispering loudly for them to open the door. He does not want to shout for fear of waking up the Talwars.

6. With Aarushi now unconscious, nothing more can be done with her. The moment of lust has passed and the two assailants are now frightened. From her condition they fear that she is very seriously injured and almost dead. They open the door. Hemraj is in a panic on seeing Aarushi unconscious, but one of his associates takes him to her, places his hand under her nose, and shows him that there is nothing to be worried about for while she is unconscious, she is still breathing.
7. The assailant is now worried that he may be identified. A frequent watcher of crime serials, he understands that identification might be possible through body fluids. In any event he realises that it makes sense to remove all evidence of Aarushi being violated sexually. He rushes to the bathroom attached to Aarushi's bedroom, gets a mug of water and a piece of cloth and tries to remove all evidence of an assault.
8. Hemraj now starts fighting with his friends. Once his friends leave all blame will naturally fall on him. They tell Hemraj to cool down. They don't want to create a ruckus discussing things loudly in Aarushi's or even in Hemraj's room, lest this wake up one of the Talwars (despite the air-conditioner) so one of them suggests they go to the terrace. I should mention here that this feeds into the Talwars' alibi that they didn't hear anything. Perhaps it would not have been possible to commit two murders in Aarushi's room without a lot of noise and commotion but because there were two assailants involved, with Aarushi's laryngitis

preventing her from screaming loudly, it *would* have been possible to have rendered her unconscious with relatively less noise.

9. Before leaving for the terrace, however, they decide to quickly tidy up Aarushi's room, even perhaps covering her neck with the bed sheet or flannel blanket. All her toys and other stuff are methodically arranged. They do this in fear of Aarushi being discovered with a serious head injury while the two assailants and Hemraj mull things over in the terrace. It is theoretically possible, they reason to themselves, that Dr Talwar may get up in the middle of night to drink some water, and decide to check in on Aarushi. He should be reassured by seeing her still sleeping peacefully, her head covered with a blanket. In addition, there should be no disorder in the room as that may arouse his suspicions. (It is worth mentioning at this juncture that Judge Lal did not consider that the killers could have been anyone other than the Talwars for the reason that the room had been evidently tidied up. As he wrote in his judgement[81]: 'An outsider killer after committing the crime will not waste his time in dressing-up the bed-sheet, arranging toys and pillow in proper order in the bed-sheet, covering the dead body of Ms. Aarushi with a flannel blanket and cleaning private parts of Ms. Aarushi as his top priority will be to escape away immediately after commission of the murder and thus dressing-up of the bed-sheet and placing toys and pillow is possible to be done by the accused persons only.')
10. On the terrace the discussion gets heated and acrimonious. Hemraj is clearly worried that unless his associates confess to the crime, or unless Aarushi regains consciousness and can speak about what happened, the suspicion will inevitably fall on him. On their part Rajkumar and Krishna

have no intention of confessing to such a serious crime; they realise that Hemraj will inevitably implicate them in order to protect himself. A fight breaks out. During the course of the fight Hemraj is hit hard with the flat end of the *khukri* and rendered unconscious. The carotid artery running past his neck is then severed with the sharp end of the blade of the *khukri*.

11. Rajkumar and Krishna then come down leaving Hemraj's dead body on the terrace. They re-enter the house using Hemraj's key, which they have taken from his pocket and decide they now have to make hundred per cent certain that Aarushi is dead. She may have been alive previously and there was a clear risk that upon recovery she would say that she had been physically and sexually assaulted (an actual rape may not have taken place in terms of penetration) which though serious would still be not as serious as a murder. However, now that Hemraj was killed, she could not be permitted to live. It's only a matter of time before Hemraj's body is discovered and if Aarushi named Rajkumar and Krishna as the persons who sexually assaulted her, it would at once be clear to anyone investigating Hemraj's death that these two were responsible not only for that crime but additionally for the murder of Hemraj. Now, they potentially faced a death sentence, and there was no way they could ever convince Aarushi not to speak. She was still unconscious from the previous blow from the *khukri* and it was a simple matter to sever her neck the same way it was done in Hemraj's case.

12. After much discussion Krishna and Rajkumar decide to stay put in NOIDA. They realise if they leave the city, they will immediately become the main suspects. The only way out for them is to stay where they are and somehow try to bluff it

out, or try and implicate the Talwars. Krishna feeds the NOIDA police fabricated stories about Rajesh's affair with Anita Durrani, the wife swapping orgies and parties that the couple attended, or even that Hemraj lusted after the young girl.

Reviewing the Alternative Scenario

There are certain plausible aspects to this scenario. In fact it could be argued there are some aspects about this theory that make it *more* plausible than the alternative theory which has the Talwars kill their daughter and the servant.

Firstly the motive for the tidying up of the bed and of the room in general seems to be much sharper and clearer with the servants than with the Talwars. The prosecution time and again emphasised the point that it could have been only the Talwars who had the time at their disposal to tidy up Aarushi's bed and the room in general. Had the killers been someone else they would have been in too much of a hurry to make their getaway to be bothered with tidying up the bed or the interiors of the room. At first look this argument does look plausible, but a closer examination overlooks it central weakness. The Talwars had time at their disposal, it is true, assuming that they were the killers but they had no reason at all to tidy up the room. The Talwars were intelligent enough to understand the implications that someone who saw a tidied-up room and bed could draw.

In terms of a motive for the tidying up of the room, a far more plausible scenario is represented in the chronology of events listed above, where before they adjourn to the terrace Hemraj and his associates decide to put the room back in a state of order to take care of the eventuality of Rajesh Talwar deciding to check in on his daughter. They were not planning on running away just then. How long would it have taken? Barely a couple of minutes.

As mentioned there in this sequence/version of events Aarushi fell unconscious with injuries to her head, but she was still alive and breathing. Hemraj, Krishna, Rajkumar and possibly Vijay Mandal adjourned to the terrace *but before they went up* they tidied up the room and bed, and possibly covered Aarushi's face and body with the flannel blanket so that if someone were to enter just by some freak chance that person would see that everything was normal and go away. To my mind, this represents a more credible motive for tidying up the bed and room – to delay discovery. It could have been done by the trio before they went to the terrace or after Rajkumar and Krishna returned to the main house; the chances are that they did this before they went up to the terrace, later on they *would* have been in too much of a hurry to get away.

After Hemraj had been killed Rajkumar and Krishna had no choice but to kill Aarushi as well because they didn't dare and try and dispose of Hemraj's body; they also knew that once Aarushi spoke about the assault, sexual or otherwise to which she was subjected, the parents would report the matter to the police, who in turn would launch a search for Hemraj; it would only be a matter of time before the body's putrid smell would render its discovery inevitable. The only chance Krishna and Rajkumar had of not being implicated in the killing of Hemraj and the assault on Aarushi was to kill the teenager as well.

Why the Associates Were More Likely Candidates to Have Severed the Arteries of Their Two Victims

Considering the circumstances of the case, there were at least three reasons why the servant's associates and not the Talwars were more likely to have decided to sever the carotid artery running past the neck of both Aarushi and Hemraj.

1. To make one hundred per cent certain that the person was dead. Yes, Krishna or Rajkumar, as

the case may be, could have thought to himself, there didn't seem to be a heartbeat and the pulse of the young girl could not be felt, but who knew? Perhaps she was still alive. There are cases reported in the newspapers now and then when a rape victim has been left for dead, but she has lived to tell the tale. Unless you were a doctor you could never be certain; better to be sure than sorry, the killer may have said to himself. And so a sure shot method was adopted to ensure the girl was dead.

2. It may have been done to implicate the Talwars. The precise, almost surgical, nature of the wounds on the neck would be certain to throw a cloud of suspicion onto the Talwars. Severing an artery is not rocket science and Krishna had years of experience assisting Rajesh Talwar in his dental clinic.
3. The weapon that was used for both the head injuries and the severing of the arteries could conceivably have been the khukri readily available in Hemraj's room. For the injuries to the head the flat end of the khukri may have been used. A nine-member team of doctors from AIIMS concluded that it was possible for the artery to have been severed by using a khukri. It was not judicious of the judge to have ruled against this opinion tendered by medical experts from the premier medical institute of the country.

Two Glasses Instead of Four

It does seem rather strange that Judge Shyam Lal could not remain consistent even when it came to appraising the credibility of a witness. The same witness is found to be credible when his deposition is helpful in convicting the Talwars, but when the evidence supports the possibility that they were innocent it is discarded as not being reliable. This is certainly the case with the testimony tendered by K.K. Gautam a former police officer who visited the Talwar residence soon after Aarushi's body was discovered. On the one hand the judge finds his statement reliable that Rajesh Talwar's brother Dinesh Kumar (also a doctor) had requested a doctor known to K.K. Gautam to see whether a reference to rape could be omitted from the post-mortem report. On the other hand the judge dismisses the statement made by the same witness when it came to a description of Hemraj's room and attached toilet. This is what Judge Shyam Lal has to say on page 165:

> *The evidence of K.K. Gautam that on examination of the room of Hemraj it was observed that three persons might have been sitting in the bed as there were depressions on the bed and in the two glasses substance like alcohol was seen and it seemed that toilet of Hemraj had not been flushed and more than one person had urinated in the toilet hardly inspires confidence as this statement is based on surmises, conjectures and speculations. It is not possible at all that in the midnight around 12.00 o'clock Krishna, Rajkumar and Vijay Mandal will come to the room of Hemraj and have liquor drinks. If it was so, four glasses might have been found there but K.K. Gautam has stated before the I.O. that in only two glasses substance like alcohol was seen which has not been confirmed by any other evidence. The prosecution story and its evidence will not receive a jerk and jolt because the erstwhile accused were not chargesheeted or put on trial as the jerk and jolt is not such as to upset and tilt the prosecution version against the accused and create any reasonable doubt in regard to their complicity in the ghastly crime. Since the occurrence is nocturnal inside the flat and the crime came into light in public domain in the morning of 16.05.2008 and therefore, it is possible in all human probability that both the accused may have created evidence of such a nature which may confuse the investigators.*
>
> A few paragraphs ahead he notes:
>
> It is also possible that whisky bottle might have been lifted after wearing gloves. It is also possible that Sula

> wine may have also been taken by the accused when he was extremely and intensely in tension after committing the crime or it was partly made empty to show that Hemraj and his friends had consumed the liquor. It is not the case of the accused that Hemraj used to take wine or liquor.

The extract is confusing. The judge discards K.K. Gautam a respected former police officer's statement all too easily.

And what is the logic? If there were four people in the room there should have been four glasses. Later in the same passage the judge concedes that Hemraj was a teetotaller so that brings the needed glass count to three. It was also not the case that all three visitors entered Hemraj's room at the same time; it's possible that Vijay Mandal was summoned only after the attack on Aarushi as depicted in the movie *Talvar*. Be that as it may, it is unlikely that all visitors to Hemraj's room that night were drinking only from a glass. One person may have grabbed a Kingfisher beer for himself (a Kingfisher bottle was also found) and sipped from it directly. Since he didn't consume alcohol, Hemraj may have been drinking from the plastic bottle of Sprite that was also discovered in this room[82]. The judge doesn't seem to have had much personal knowledge with respect to the consumption of alcohol. This possibly led him to draw the bona fide, but erroneous, conclusion that beer or wine will typically be drunk only in a glass, or to even understand that some people prefer wine, and others beer. Certainly the judge reveals his drinking inexperience and ignorance on alcohol related matters when he suggests that '*it is also possible that Sula wine may have also been taken by the accused when he was extremely and intensely in tension after committing the crime*'. Is Judge Shyam Lal endorsing Sula wine as being more potent than a whisky for Rajesh Talwar to have consumed it in preference to a hypothetical double Scotch when he was 'extremely and intensely in tension'.

Although the Japanese are said to drink wine mixed with Scotch, it is relatively uncommon for a mature drinker in India, which Dr Rajesh Talwar undoubtedly was, to start mixing whisky with wine because of tension; he would make himself a stiffer peg or down an extra couple of pegs. The other thing is that why would he keep the bottle of Sula wine in Hemraj's room, while keeping the bottle of Scotch on the table in the living room. That there was one glass less discovered in Hemraj's room doesn't make the drinking improbable in the least or become grounds to simply dismiss the statement of K. K. Gautam regarding the depression on the bed and the filthy state of the toilet as evidence of a drinking party in session. He writes in his judgement that K.K. Gautam's evidence 'hardly inspires confidence as this statement is based on surmises, conjectures and speculations'. However, with circumstantial evidence as the only kind of evidence available in this case, Judge Lal too has drawn up his guilty verdict based on similar 'surmises, conjectures and speculations'.

The judge even goes on to suggest that Dr Rajesh Talwar may have planted the bottles and glasses in Hemraj's room, just as he might have carefully, wearing gloves planted the Ballantine Scotch whisky bottle on the table. Why would he do this? Why didn't he plant a glass next to the bottle of Ballantine Scotch found on the dining table?

A lesson for Dr Rajesh Talwar (assuming he was innocent) was that one should never shout at your underlings if you have a young girl in the house. An uncle of mine who has three young daughters is constantly reminded of this by his wife: 'Keep your temper in check,' she says, 'and don't lose your cool on people. Never ever forget there are three young girls in the house....' If the scenario described in this part of this book is correct and it was Hemraj's associates who committed the murders, more especially if it was Krishna the compounder who was the prime motivator then while his attraction for

Aarushi may have caused his assault on her, an added motivation of revenge against the father, may have also figured.

Twenty-seven Reasons Why Hemraj's Associates Committed the Murders

There is a profound quotation that I use by Sherlock Holmes at the outset of the first part of the book. It is worth repeating at this juncture.

> '*Circumstantial evidence is a very tricky thing, ... It may serve to point very straight to one thing, but if you shift your own point of view a little, you may find it pointing in an equally uncompromising manner to something entirely different*'.

So, just a slight shift and someone else starts to appear guilty. Judge Shyam Lal listed twenty-six reasons why he was convinced that the Talwars were guilty. I am happy to provide one extra reason why Hemraj's associates committed the murders. I believe my reasons are far more convincing than Judge Shyam Lal's reasons and aside from the occasional 'mere', I have also tried to use a similar style.

1. The statement of K.K. Gautam, a former police officer with great experience needs to be trusted, as he has no reason not to be telling the truth. In his statement to the police he has divulged important information with respect to the state of Hemraj's room on the night of the killings. He stated that the mattress on Hemraj's bed was depressed suggesting that a number of people were sitting on it. In addition he has testified to the presence of empty beer bottles, an empty bottle of Sula wine, and empty glasses. It is also a matter of record that the deceased Hemraj was a teetotaller and never consumed liquor. It therefore goes without saying that there was clearly a party in progress that night.

2. Rajesh Talwar and his wife Nupur Talwar were middle-aged professionals. Sometimes extreme situations give you immense strength, but it is less likely that after a gruelling day at work they would have had the energy or strength to carry Hemraj's body to the terrace. It is far more likely that Hemraj accompanied his associates to the terrace, as there was the risk of their loud arguments waking up the Talwars. It is possible (though less likely) that Hemraj was wounded in Aarushi's room itself having been attacked with the blunt side of the khukri and his associates carried his unconscious body to the terrace where his neck was severed with the khukri.
3. The compounder Krishna had a clear motive for sexually violating Aarushi Talwar. In this way he would not only be able to satisfy his lust, but simultaneously have his revenge against his employer for the shouting and humiliation he had received only the previous week. Ms Anita Durrani stated how a few days before the attack Dr Rajesh Talwar had shouted at Krishna for not preparing a cast properly and humiliated him in his clinic in the presence of patients.
4. A highly qualified team of medical professionals from the country's prestigious All India Institute of Medical Sciences issued an opinion that it was possible to inflict the injuries found on deceased Aarushi and Hemraj's neck by the use of a khukri. This is not the case of an individual doctor deposing at the behest of the prosecution such as Dr Raj or a doctor appearing on behalf of the defence such as Dr Urmila, but a committee of independent medical professionals whose opinion can safely, and without doubt, be respected.
5. It is likely that Hemraj had visitors late at night. During the course of the day he was busy working for the Talwars. It was only after the family would

retire for the night that he would get the chance to socialise. So it is highly likely that he had Rajkumar and Krishna visit him in his room.

6. It was also possible for Hemraj to let his friends into his room directly, as his room opened into the passage. It is true that a fridge was placed against that door, but it would not have been a difficult task to move the fridge slightly, in order to let a visitor directly into his room. Alternatively he could just open the front door and have them enter the house through the main entrance. The Talwars were busy professionals, and the loud air conditioner in their room meant that they would not notice if someone rang the bell and entered the house.
7. It is not true as observed by Judge Shyam Lal that Krishna and Rajkumar would not have dared to consume alcohol in Hemraj's room. It is a matter of record that empty bottles of alcohol and glasses were found in his room.
8. It may be true that in their normal state Krishna and Rajkumar would not have dared to sexually violate Aarushi. However, it has been proved time and over that alcohol does make people indulge in the most vile crimes.
9. It is clear that Hemraj's associates consumed a fair amount of alcohol, as ex-police officer K.K. Gautam informed the investigators that the toilet adjoining Hemraj's servant room was found to be in a stinking state. It is not credible that the Talwars would use their servant's toilet in order to make it stink, and create the impression of a party where none had taken place.
10. No motive could be ascribed to the Talwars for killing their only daughter other than Dr Rajesh Talwar suddenly discovering his daughter in a compromising position with the servant. Hemraj was a grandfather with grandchildren. Even the

thought of having sexual relations with Aarushi would not have crossed his mind. It is far more likely that Hemraj's associates, who were younger and drunk at the time, committed the crime. One of them had been humiliated by Dr Rajesh Talwar only the previous week and may have been feeling vengeful.

11. Hemraj could not have thought of Aarushi in terms other than being his employer's daughter, or indeed someone akin to his own daughter. Moreover, he was a teetotaller so there was no question of his morality being 'loosened' in any way. This could, however, have credibly happened to his associates.
12. It is not credible that a young, attractive teenager like Aarushi would be physically intimate with the family servant. The mere thought of such a thing would surely have disgusted and revolted her.
13. Aarushi was a beautiful girl with male friends her own age. It is a matter of record that on the night of the murder itself a boy tried to call her first on her mobile and then later on the landline.
14. Even if for the sake of argument we accept that Aarushi and Hemraj were discovered in a sexually compromising situation, would the two have not taken the precaution of at least shutting the door especially since it had an auto locking system? However, A.G.L. Kaul, CBI Team Two's investigating officer stated that in his view the door leading to Aarushi's bedroom had been left open. Judge Shyam Lal expressed a different view in his judgement not realising that further explanations would become necessary if the door *was* in fact locked. Would Rajesh Talwar not then simply knock on Aarushi's door and ask her to open it? It is true that in an interview Nupur Talwar stated that she may have inadvertently left the key in the latch itself[83], and therefore there would have been

no need for him to knock, but even assuming for a minute that Aarushi and Hemraj were intending to be intimate, would they not have taken the elementary precaution of not only shutting the door but of removing the key that had been left in the keyhole. And if the door was locked and the key removed beforehand, a fairly routine precaution, forcing Dr Rajesh Talwar to knock would that not give enough time for Aarushi and Hemraj to disengage? There was after all, no reason for Rajesh Talwar to enter Aarushi's room in the middle of the night. The idea that he woke up in the middle of the night and used the key to enter Aarushi's bedroom (without any reason to do so) boggles the mind. Further, the idea that Aarushi and Hemraj did not hear him turning the key and continued to remain sexually engaged strains credulity yet further.

15. The Talwars were a modern, cosmopolitan couple. Even if Dr Rajesh Talwar had found the servant in a compromising position with his daughter, it is not credible that he would fly into a rage and attempt to kill Hemraj. It is still less credible that while attempting to attack or kill Hemraj, he should have accidentally killed his own daughter.
16. Both Rajesh Talwar and Nupur Talwar were subjected to a second polygraph test, as the first test did not reveal anything.[84] Nothing remotely incriminating surfaced despite the repeated tests to which they were subjected.[85] On the other hand in the polygraph tests of Krishna, an associate of Hemraj he was judged to be 'deceptive and manipulative' and 'loyal to no one.'[86]
17. Both Hemraj and Krishna made revelatory statements during the course of the narco-tests. The Talwars were made to undergo the same tests by CBI Team Two but they passed the tests without

any suspicions being raised about their responses to questioning while under the effect of the drug.

18. The wet bed sheet clearly shows that the assailants attempted to wipe all signs of their assault on Aarushi. According to the CFSL report expert opinion established the 'presence of a wet circular mark on the bed sheet below the pelvic area of Aarushi which was not urine'.[87]
19. Records show that not a single drop of Hemraj's blood was discovered in Aarushi's bedroom. This makes it pretty clear that his artery was severed on the terrace. It is very credible that Hemraj accompanied his associates to the terrace where a scuffle broke out and he was murdered. The thought of the Talwars carrying an injured but not dead Hemraj to the terrace (where they would sever his artery) seems far less credible because there would be a possibility of the injured and presumably unconscious Hemraj reviving and fighting back. Secondly, if the objective was to kill Hemraj why make it such a bloody messy affair? On the other hand Hemraj's associates needed the certitude of death, which a severed artery would provide.
20. The severing of an artery does not in itself require advanced medical knowledge. This may have been accomplished by Krishna who had assisted Rajesh Talwar in many surgeries for a considerable period of time.
21. The Talwars had no motive to kill their daughter. Judge Lal too concedes that the motive was difficult to establish but he still went ahead and convicted them. The rumours of wife swapping and Rajesh Talwar's alleged relationship with Dr Anita Durrani were baseless and were never subsequently verified, only serving to sully the reputation of the Talwars and turn public opinion against them. These were rumours that were created by the Krishna-

Rajkumar duo and fed to the investigators in order to divert attention from their own role.

22. The room was found tidied up. The Talwars had no motive to tidy up the room. On the other hand, after hitting Aarushi with the blunt end of the khukri and rendering her unconscious, Krishna and Rajkumar became worried that their arguing might awaken the Talwars. They were also worried that while on the terrace and hurriedly deciding what they should do next, Dr Rajesh Talwar might check on his daughter and discover that she had been violated and was unconscious. They therefore decided to rearrange the room and make it tidy once again in order to potentially delay discovery of the crime.
23. It is also possible that the room was tidied up because Rajkumar and Krishna were still debating whether they should flee NOIDA. Although Aarushi would have been discovered by the morning, tidying up the room might help ensure that discovery would be delayed while they hotfooted it back to their villages in Nepal. Eventually though they realised that there was no direct evidence implicating them, and therefore decided it would be better to stay. If they suddenly disappeared it would be perceived as a sign of guilt, and they would become the prime suspects for both the killings. Realising this, they decided to stay on in NOIDA and bluff it out.
24. It is a matter of record that Nupur Talwar tried to telephone Hemraj on his mobile in the morning when the maid, Bharti Mandal arrived at the house. It is also a matter of record that the phone rang before it was switched off. It was subsequently discovered that the phone rang in the NOIDA area. This makes it clear that it was the associates of Hemraj and no one else who could have committed the murders.

25. The third accused, Vijay Mandal spoke during the narco-test of how he came to the Talwar residence and learnt about the murders. Mandal was sought to be made an approver by CBI Team One, but the idea was eventually abandoned. Had Team One continued to remain in charge there is every possibility that Krishna and Rajkumar, the real culprits would have been prosecuted and eventually punished.
26. Hemraj fetched the bottle of Ballantine for his friends. It may have been an idea to replace the depleted contents with water or other cheap liquor the next day while the Talwars were away at work. It was a fair assumption for Hemraj to make that Dr Rajesh Talwar would not check his stock of liquor till the evening of the following day.
27. There was a fingerprint discovered on the bottle of Ballantine whisky, which did not match the fingerprints of either of the Talwars. That fingerprint could also not be successfully matched with either Hemraj or any of his associates. This suggests that there was a third person present at the crime scene, one that has not been identified till date. The only credible possibility is that it was yet another unidentified associate of Hemraj. This associate may have also teamed up with Rajkumar and Krishna to commit the crimes. No other credible explanation for that fingerprint exists.

The So-Called Additional Evidence Against the Three Suspects

The so-called forensic evidence coupled with expert opinion concerned all three suspects, namely Rajkumar, Krishna and Vijay Mandal. CBI Team One concluded that either Krishna or Rajkumar, or both, were the killers. It was envisaged that Vijay Mandal could become an approver. The polygraph, narco-evidence and expert opinion against Krishna and Rajkumar was therefore more important.

KRISHNA, THE COMPOUNDER

The Polygraph

The director of the Central Forensic Science Laboratory (CFSL), Ms Bibha Rani Ray herself conducted the polygraph test on Krishna. Ms Ray and other behavioural experts came to the conclusion that Krishna was being 'deceptive and manipulative'. He was shifting blame on to others and 'was loyal to no one'.[88]

The Narco-tests

Krishna's narco test was a dead give-away. He is alleged to have spilled details of the crime and the weapon used. Crucially, he went on to say that a) he, Rajkumar and Vijay Mandal were all present in the flat at midnight; b) Dr Rajesh Talwar had nothing to do with the murders; and c) he witnessed Rajkumar committing the crime.

Following this test CBI Team One raided the servant's quarters of L-14 Jalvayu Vihar and recovered a khukri with specks of blood on it and a blood-stained purple pillow cover.[89]

> *Some additional forensic evidence appeared against Krishna. The murdered servant Hemraj's DNA was discovered in traces of blood that were discovered on Krishna's purple pillow cover.*[90] *This was the only direct evidence linking Krishna to the crime, and could have clinched the case against him and Rajkumar.*

However, subsequently this turned out to be a typographical error.

RAJKUMAR

Rajkumar worked for the Durranis, also dentists living in Jalvayu Vihar, NOIDA. He was younger than Krishna and good-looking. Some time back, Aarushi had given her cell phone to Vidushi, her friend (daughter of the Durranis) who in turn gave it to Rajkumar.

If Krishna was found to be 'deceptive and manipulative' Dr Vaya who conducted the polygraph on Rajkumar found him to be 'fidgety and uncooperative'. Why should anyone have expected him to be cooperative? After all, it was not clear that he had gone in for these tests willingly. The other thing is that he was clearly fearful of being implicated and is reported to have said something on the lines of '*Ismey main phas to nahi jaoonga,*' or 'I hope I will not be trapped as a result of these tests.'

Under the influence of drugs administered during the narco-tests Rajkumar made the following statements: (a) that they were drinking; (b) that they watched TV and listened to Nepali songs on a certain channel; (c) there was a fight between Hemraj and Krishna; (d) Hemraj admonished Krishna and told him that he would wake up everyone; and (e) it was Krishna who had committed the murders.

So, in other words neither Krishna nor Rajkumar confessed to having carried out the murders even in the narco tests. Krishna said Rajkumar had done the killing and Rajkumar blamed Krishna. Neither blamed the third associate Vijay Mandal.

VIJAY MANDAL

The third suspect, Vijay Mandal was employed with Puneesh Tandon, a neighbour of the Talwars and lived in a garage (L-28, Sector 25).

Subjected to a similar narco testing he revealed:

(a) That all three were together at the Talwar's flat together with Hemraj that fateful night;

(b) There was a struggle with Aarushi; and

(c) He became fearful after her killing

CBI Team One suspected Hemraj's associates and believed the Talwars to be innocent. It was clearly influenced by the results of the above tests, even though these were not admissible in court. It was felt that the best way forward was to get Vijay Mandal to confess (to) being there and implicate Rajkumar and Krishna in the killings.[91]

Confessions Under Police Torture

Not unsurprisingly, given the widespread use of third degree in the country the police adopted the age-old method of conducting investigations into crime: third degree treatment, or in other words torture. On several occasions the investigators sought police remand where they could interrogate and torture Krishna and Rajkumar to gain some proof or evidence against them. The orders passed by the magistrate on 17 June 2008 with respect to the extension of Krishna's remand read as follows[92]: 'CBI has produced the case diary which has been perused by this court, the arguments contained in the case diaries have also been perused .... Accused Krishna has admitted and confessed to be involved in the double murders .... In the night of 15.5.2008, at around 12.00, he had gone to meet Hemraj. He has also admitted that he can get recovered the mobile phone of Aarushi'.

Ten days later, on 27 June 2008 the magistrate passed a similar order regarding Rajkumar's arrest and alleged confession: 'Case diary has been perused. The statement of accused [Rajkumar] has also been perused in which he confessed that he switched off Aarushi's mobile phone, broke it, and concealed it, which he can get recovered. He can also get recovered Hemraj's mobile'.

Statements Without Police Torture and Narco-Tests

Outside the tests, however, in a fully conscious state, and without being subjected to police torture, both Krishna and Rajkumar denied that they had been together drinking in Hemraj's room in the Talwars' flat. Each claimed to have been home and asleep. Vijay Mandal's employers provided an alibi that he was asleep by 9.30 pm.[93]

A Major Error in the Forensic Laboratory

There is a scene in the film *Talvar* that goes wrong, terribly wrong. The CBI investigating officer, Arun Kumar is proceeding with the prosecution of Krishna and Rajkumar when the new director of the CBI questions what real proof he has against the associates of the dead servant, narco-tests not being admissible in a court of law. Arun Kumar replies that there is a DNA match – Hemraj's blood has been discovered on a purple pillow cover seized from the then accused Krishna's room. A few days later when this is sought to be double-checked it turns out to be a typographical error! Sen's book *Aarushi* also refers to this anomaly and raises the question of how that very same typing error was repeated multiple times.

The film subtly suggests that the earlier reports were accurate and the discovery of the typographical error was manufactured. (This can of course happen theoretically, but there was no evidence that it did). Given that this was the only piece of direct evidence linking Hemraj's associates with the crime, the prosecution case against them came apart at the seams. Circumstantial evidence still remained.

This suggestion is incredulous. Of course, DIG Arun Kumar was devastated and the needle of suspicion now shifted back to the Talwars under the directions of the new CBI director. The point is that the CFSL had no reason to be telling lies. A.G.L. Kaul may not have been the most scrupulous of investigators but this is an unfair accusation to level against him: that he somehow conspired with the forensic authorities. It stretches the bounds of credulity to suggest that Kaul was so dead set against the Talwars he decided to have the associates of Hemraj exonerated. It was not even his decision to make but that of forensics. It may be true that national forensic laboratories in the country (and elsewhere in the world) come under the influence of investigative agencies but it is not at all credible that they would go to the extent of denying a

DNA match where one existed! After all, forensics would have received great credit for its work in nailing the culprits, despite contamination of the crime scene. An error was made, and the error was discovered, well in time. No one would have wanted innocent servants to suffer instead of the innocent parents. And all are innocent in the eyes of the law, until and unless they are proved guilty beyond 'all reasonable doubt'. Neither is this the first time or place that such an error has happened. It would also not be the last.

A report in *The Independent* refers to such situations. In the context of forensic testing in private laboratories it reported how one person 'was behind a mix-up at its main laboratory that led to an innocent man being wrongly accused of rape for months'. The same lab 'was also criticised after a typing error resulted in police chasing an unidentified suspect in the "spy-in-the-bag" death case of MI6 man Gareth Williams'. It later emerged that the DNA came from a police scientist.[94]

Innocents have also been trapped because of human error, which nearly happened in the Aarushi case as well. The same report noted how 'the arrest of an innocent man for rape because of a mix-up over DNA samples has previously led to calls for an inquiry into the closure of the Forensic Science Service'. The facts in that case are stated below:

> *Adam Scott was arrested and held in custody for five months over an allegation of rape even though he was hundreds of miles away from the scene of the crime.*
>
> *His DNA had been retrieved from a "spitting incident" in Exeter but became mixed up during the analysis of genetic material taken from a rape victim in Manchester.*
>
> *The problems were attributed to "human error" at the headquarters of LGC forensics, when a plastic tray containing a sample of Mr Scott's DNA was wrongly*

re-used for the analysis of a swab taken from the rape victim.

He was charged in October 2011 based on the DNA evidence and was not released until the following March. Mobile-phone records backed up his story that he was 280 miles away at the time of the attack.

On the other hand, DNA testing can sometimes trump other inaccurate forensic testing. In the US there was the tragic case of Ron Williamson and Dennis Fritz. These two individuals were both convicted for a rape and murder that they did not commit due to inaccurate and misleading forensic evidence. Each spent over a decade a jail. Their families and loved ones suffered too, as is inevitably the case. Dennis Fritz was a high school teacher and a single parent. Williamson, who received a harsher sentence and was even on death row, had been a star baseball player. In their case DNA testing established the weakness of forensic analysis of hair left at the crime scene and ultimately led to their exoneration and release.[95]

There is also the case of Brandon Moon in the United States who was convicted for a rape that he did not commit due to the erroneous testimony of a forensic analyst. The Justice Project notes how 'the botched handling of post-conviction DNA testing kept Moon in prison for seventeen years before he was ultimately exonerated'.[96] After the tests and analyses were complete in 2004, Brandon Moon was finally freed from prison after seventeen years of wrongful incarceration. An apology was issued by the district attorney of El Paso in the following terms: 'I would like to convey my apologies to Mr Moon on behalf of the State of Texas and acknowledge that an apology at this time is inadequate...'[97]

More about the Narco-Tests

It is clear enough that truth serum was not administered to the subjects willingly. Evidence to this effect has emerged in social media clearly suggesting that pressure was being put on the servants to get them to confess to the crime.

A report in the *Asian Age* newspaper on 26 October 2015 explains the position somewhat.[9]

> *In a new twist to Aarushi-Hemraj murder case, it has emerged that the CBI does not have complete raw footage of narco-analysis conducted on Krishna, an assistant of Aarushi's father Rajesh Talwar, in its records. Agency reports quoted CBI sources as saying that the bureau has only about 45 minutes of video of the test conducted on Krishna in its records at Forensic Science Laboratory in Bengaluru.*

The new video is almost an hour long. This means that if it is genuine, roughly fifteen minutes of the original video was deleted. Since in any case the video was not admissible as evidence in court, what was the need then to delete almost one-fourth of the entire length? Who deleted those fifteen minutes? The deleted sections did not show the CBI investigators in a favourable light. Perhaps someone hoped that the video *would* be somehow eventually admissible in court, and deleted sections that showed Krishna and Rajkumar to be in a vulnerable position.

The report goes on to state[99]:

> *The apparent raw footage of the tests, which has emerged, shows Krishna claiming that the then CBI joint director Arun Kumar had asked him to own the crime on the promise of a reduced sentence. Kumar had said the "original" footage did not have that portion.*

The video posted on YouTube on 22 October 2015 is 58.55 minutes long – so just a minute and five seconds short of a full hour. The person who posted the video claimed that another part would soon be made public. If this is true, then the deletions were longer than one-fourth of the entire footage.

The CBI has been quizzed by the media about the discrepancy in length between the two videos. It does seem unlikely that someone could go to the length of manufacturing a video with the same actors in it. The CBI claims to be clueless about who edited the video, whether it was the doctors that did the tests, the person who created the CDs or officers of their own investigation team. [100]

Another report in the *Hindustan Times* speaks of how Rajesh Talwar's aide Krishna was pressurised by the CBI to make a confession. According to this news report[101]

> *Krishna Thadarai, former medical assistant of dentist Rajesh Talwar, has allegedly said in a video that he was asked by the CBI's former joint director Arun Kumar to own up to the double murder of Talwars' daughter Aarushi and their domestic help Hemraj.*
>
> *The video was purportedly recorded during a narco analysis test conducted on Thadarai after his arrest in June 2008. Narco test findings are not admissible in courts.*
>
> *Thadarai purportedly claimed in the video that the officer had promised him a reduced sentence if he owned up to the murders.*
>
> *'I have not committed any crime. I had told them the first time when they had asked me to take the allegations on myself,' Thadarai had said while responding to the queries of a medical expert during the test in the video. When the doctor asked Thadarai about who had asked him to implicate himself, Krishna said, 'IG Kumar'.*

There is the important juristic concept that the courts should not savour the 'fruits of a poisonous tree'. Confessions in custodial situations fall into that category. Testimony under narco tests is unreliable in itself but if there is a threating aspect to it, or the suggestion of force, or even inducement, this becomes yet another reason why the self incriminating testimony given under narco-tests ought not to be considered in law. Indian law has incorporated this idea in its criminal law under several provisions.[102]

What a Narco-Test Can, and Cannot, Reveal

On the issue of a narco test, this is what the CIA that practically invented the use of this serum has to say about what it can, and cannot, reveal:

> *The salient points that emerge from this discussion are the following. No such magic brew as the popular notion of truth serum exists. The barbiturates, by disrupting defensive patterns, may sometimes be helpful in interrogation, but even under the best conditions they will elicit an output contaminated by deception, fantasy, garbled speech, etc. A major vulnerability they produce in the subject is a tendency to believe he has revealed more than he has. It is possible, however, for both normal individuals and psychopaths to resist drug interrogation; it seems likely that any individual who can withstand ordinary intensive interrogation can hold out in narcosis. The best aid to a defense against narco-interrogation is foreknowledge of the process and its limitations. There is an acute need for controlled experimental studies of drug reaction, not only to depressants but also to stimulants and to combinations of depressants, stimulants, and ataraxics...*[103]

The paper by George Bimmerle, approved by the CIA, and displayed on its website goes on to state in clear terms how:

> *The notion of drugs capable of illuminating hidden recesses of the mind, helping to heal the mentally ill and preventing or reversing the miscarriage of justice, has provided an exceedingly durable theme for the press and popular literature. While acknowledging that "truth serum" is a misnomer twice over " the drugs are not sera and they do not necessarily bring forth probative truth " journalistic accounts continue to exploit the appeal of the term. The formula is to play up a few spectacular*

"truth" drug successes and to imply that the drugs are more maligned than need be and more widely employed in criminal investigation than can officially be admitted.[104]

Why the Supreme Court Does Not Permit Polygraphs and Narco Tests to be used as Evidence in Court

The public, however, is not fully informed by the media about how the polygraph (lie detector test) and narco-test work, and why the courts cannot accept these tests as evidence. At the risk of introducing some bare facts, let us try and understand the reasoning of the Supreme Court.

As a matter of fact narco testing has only recently started to be used in India (the Ajmal Kasab case being one such high profile case where it was used; Kasab was the only gunman to be caught alive in the aftermath of the 26/11 terrorist attacks in Mumbai). The Supreme Court has considered this matter in some detail in the case of *Selvi versus State of Karnataka.*[105] It is worth quoting directly from the judgement to explain why the Supreme Court, in its wisdom, did not permit these tests to be admitted into evidence, *even if they were voluntary.*

Legal questions arose in a batch of criminal appeals that all related to 'the involuntary administration of certain scientific techniques, namely narcoanalysis, polygraph examination and the Brain Electrical Activation Profile (BEAP) test for the purpose of improving investigation efforts in criminal cases'.[106]

The question of liberties being infringed is one aspect of the matter; the other issue is how useful are these tests on their own in providing proof of the commission of a crime.

The Polygraph or Lie Detector Test

On the issue of polygraph testing the Supreme Court observed:[107]

Polygraph tests have several limitations and therefore a margin for errors. The premise behind these tests is questionable because the measured changes in physiological responses are not necessarily triggered by lying or deception. Instead, they could be triggered by nervousness, anxiety, fear, confusion or other emotions. Furthermore, the physical conditions in the polygraph examination room can also create distortions in the recorded responses. The test is best administered in comfortable surroundings where there are no potential distractions for the subject and complete privacy is maintained. The mental state of the subject is also vital since a person in a state of depression or hyperactivity is likely to offer highly disparate physiological responses which could mislead the examiner. In some cases the subject may have suffered from loss of memory in the intervening time-period between the relevant act and the conduct of the test. When the subject does not remember the facts in question, there will be no self-awareness of truth or deception and hence the recording of the physiological responses will not be helpful. Errors may also result from 'memory-hardening', i.e. a process by which the subject has created and consolidated false memories about a particular incident. This commonly occurs in respect of recollections of traumatic events and the subject may not be aware of the fact that he/she is lying.

Paragraph 17: The errors associated with polygraph tests are broadly grouped into two categories, i.e., 'false positives' and 'false negatives'. A 'false positive' occurs when the results indicate that a person has been deceitful even though he/she answered truthfully. Conversely a 'false negative' occurs when a set of deceptive responses is reported as truthful.

The most serious concern with polygraphs though is that a clever subject can also manipulate the tests to his own advantage. The Supreme Court observed:

However, the biggest concern about polygraph tests is that an examiner may not be able to recognise deliberate attempts on part of the subject to manipulate the test results. Such 'countermeasures' are techniques which are deliberately used by the subject to create certain physiological responses in order to deceive the examiner. The intention is that by deliberately enhancing one's reaction to the control questions, the examiner will incorrectly score the test in favour of truthfulness rather than deception. The most commonly used 'countermeasures' are those of creating a false sense of mental anxiety and stress at the time of the interview, so that the responses triggered by lying cannot be readily distinguished.

The British Psychological Society (BPS) also came to a similar conclusion. In its report it made the following succinct observation[108]:

A polygraph is sometimes called a lie detector, but this term is misleading. A polygraph does not detect lies, but only arousal which is assumed to accompany telling a lie.

Narco-tests

The court pointed out the limitations of the naroanalysis technique in these terms[109]:

It is also important to be aware of the limitations of the 'narcoanalysis' technique. It does not have an absolute success rate and there is always the possibility that the subject will not reveal any relevant information. Some studies have shown that most of the drug-induced revelations are not related to the relevant facts and they are more likely to be in the nature of inconsequential information about the subjects' personal lives. It takes great skill on part of the interrogators to extract and identify information which could eventually prove to be useful. While some persons are able to retain their ability to deceive even in the hypnotic state, others can become

> *extremely suggestible to questioning. This is especially worrying, since investigators who are under pressure to deliver results could frame questions in a manner that prompts incriminatory responses. Subjects could also concoct fanciful stories in the course of the 'hypnotic stage'. Since the responses of different individuals are bound to vary, there are* 49 *no uniform criteria for evaluating the efficacy of the 'narcoanalysis' technique.*

The constitutional prohibition to the use of narcoanalysis is that it violated the privacy rights of an individual technique. What about when a person willingly goes in for the testing, as was the case with the Talwars. Everyone easily understands the argument that no one should be forced to incriminate himself, but some argue that surely the Talwars should be permitted to prove their innocence on the basis of their excellent and non-incriminatory results in the narco tests. In my view as clearly outlined in this book there was no case against the Talwars and therefore they should have been acquitted. Their performance during the narco tests is irrelevant. It is also not the case that it is only because of some legal technicality they are not permitted to be used *even to establish innocence.* The US courts have been seized of this matter for much longer than we have in India. In *State v. Lindemuth*, 56 N.M. 237 (1952) the testimony of a psychiatrist was not admitted when he wanted to prove that answers given by a defendant under the influence of sodium pentothal supported the defendant's plea of innocence in a murder case.

Medical Ethics

Of course doctors match blood, sputum and semen without permission of any of the suspects, and none of this is illegal, but 'testimony' that can be used to incriminate someone stands on a different footing altogether. As the Supreme Court noted in the *Selvi* case (para 156):

Fields such as forensic toxicology have become important in criminal-justice systems all over the world and doctors are frequently called on to examine bodily substances such as samples of blood, hair, semen, saliva, sweat, sputum and fingernail clippings as well as marks, wounds and other physical characteristics. A reasonable limitation on the forensic uses of medical expertise is the fact that testimonial acts such as the results of a psychiatric examination cannot be used as evidence without the subject's informed consent. Results of impugned tests should be treated as 'personal testimony'.

Informed Consent

Interestingly the Supreme Court also pointed out (para 202) how: *'it is also quite conceivable that an individual may give his/her consent to undergo the said tests on account of threats, false promises or deception by the investigators. For example, a person may be convinced to give his/her consent after being promised that this would lead to an early release from custody or dropping of charges. However, after the administration of the tests the investigators may renege on such promises. In such a case the relevant inquiry is not confined to the apparent voluntariness of the act of undergoing the tests, but also includes an examination of the totality of circumstances'.*

What Purpose Does a Narco-Test Serve if it is Inadmissible as Evidence in Court?

The reader will no doubt question what the purpose of conducting a narco-test is if it is inadmissible as evidence in the courts? A narco-test is not admissible but it is possible it may lead to the discovery of material that can be used as evidence. As the Supreme Court observed there is 'of course a very real possibility that information extracted through such interviews **can lead to the uncovering of independent evidence which may be relevant**.' *(Emphasis author)*[110] If the test results enable investigators to discover independent materials that are relevant to a case, surely such subsequently discovered materials should be admissible during trial?

The answer to this question is: yes, and no, or it depends. Remember that juristic remark about the fruits of a poisonous tree.

The court ruled on this important issue as follows[111]:

We hold that no individual should be forcibly subjected to any of the techniques in question, whether in the context of investigation in criminal cases or otherwise. Doing so would amount to an unwarranted intrusion into personal liberty. However, we do leave room for the voluntary administration of the impugned techniques in the context of criminal justice, provided that certain safeguards are in place. Even when the subject has given consent to undergo any of these tests, the test results by themselves cannot be admitted as evidence because the subject does not exercise conscious control over the responses during the administration of the test. However, any information or material that is subsequently discovered with the help of voluntary administered test results can be admitted.

The point to be noted is that the subsequent material discovered is admissible in court only if the narco testing on the subjects was voluntary. In the case of Krishna and Rajkumar, there was a huge question mark over the alleged voluntary nature of the tests administered to them.

Be that as it may, *in any case* there was nothing, not a scrap of tangible, direct evidence that was discovered subsequent to the testimony (which itself was of a forced nature). Following the narco-test, had Hemraj or Aarushi's mobile, or a murder weapon, or blood-stained clothes of the killer, anything, had been recovered, it could all have been admissible in court, provided the narco-tests were conducted voluntarily.

So Should Have Hemraj's Associates Been Convicted?

A little earlier in this section of the book I provided twenty-seven reasons why Hemraj's associates were guilty, and I believe them to be more convincing than the twenty-six reasons provided by Judge Shyam Lal in his judgement. There is also the so-called additional evidence that influenced CBI Team One. The Talwars did not say anything that could possibly be held against them in the polygraph test conducted by CBI Team One as well as in the narco-tests conducted by CBI Team Two. On the other hand the associates of Hemraj did make statements in these tests that deserved closer scrutiny, and appeared evasive on the one hand, and involved in the crime, on the other hand. This evidence is, however, not admissible for perfectly sensible reasons just discussed.

Despite the twenty-seven reasons I provided in favour of the guilt of Krishna and Rajkumar, it does not mean that I believe that these reasons taken cumulatively cross the threshold of 'reasonable doubt', a mandatory requirement under the law before a person can be convicted of a crime. It does not matter what I personally or anyone else believes; the point is that people cannot be incarcerated for the commission of crimes based on evidence that does not satisfy the criteria of 'beyond all reasonable doubt'.

It is certainly possible that Krishna and Rajkumar committed the murders. In terms of the requirements of the law, however, which are there for a reason, their conviction cannot be legally sustained. Someone might even argue that it is not only 'possible' it is 'plausible' that the duo, or trio as the case may be (if we include Vijay Mandal) committed the murders; that too is not sufficient. In the end I do not believe that my twenty-seven reasons can sustain a conviction against Hemraj's associates any more than the twenty-six reasons advanced by Judge Shyam Lal could sustain a conviction against the Talwars.

Logic, as a philosopher once famously said, can be a whore.

Part - Three

Someone Else Killed Aarushi and Hemraj

This is a court of law, young man, not a court of justice.
— Oliver Wendell Holmes, Jr.

CONFESSION TO A MURDER THAT WASN'T

(*A teenage crush ends up tragically with two people accidentally dead and everyone thinks it was murder*)

I suppose I should make a clean breast of it, but I can't. It's true that two innocents may spend a lifetime of incarcerated suffering unless I make a confession, but if I do speak out it will not be prison alone, but could well be my neck that will be placed in the noose.

My hands tremble as I write this, but I have to put it down. It's the only way I know of giving vent to what happened that terrible night and unload a dark secret that that has caused me such agony. After all, I cannot speak about it to anyone, not even my mother.

It's not that I haven't taken a life before I took hers and the servant's, but I can in all honesty say that I had never before killed or even seriously injured a single human being. I have dissected rats and cockroaches and once I ran over a dog when I took Dad's old Fiat out for a spin. Those dissections took place because I was a premedical student anxious to gain admission to a medical college.

Let me rewind. These ghastly events took place roughly seven years ago when I lived with my mother in the DDA flats in Mayur Vihar. We had moved there recently from Maurice Nagar following the unexpected and premature death of my father, a professor at Delhi University.

* * *

I first saw her standing near the bus stop just near G block, which is where I lived. The metro had only recently been introduced, and many of us were still taking buses. That day, as fate would have it, we were the only two people waiting for a bus. I was waiting for bus number sixty-three that would take me all the way to Hindu college at Delhi University, where I was a first year student pursuing Zoo *Oh*, or Zoology Honours. The idea at the time was to give a few medical college entrance tests and hopefully get a seat in one of the better ones. I was determined to become a doctor.

The young girl with large innocent eyes was wearing a dark-blue pleated skirt and a white top. Clearly a schoolgirl. I hadn't been out of school that long myself; there was possibly only a difference of a couple of years between us. She did look as if she was going to finish school soon.

I saw her but didn't dwell on her much, my attention being focussed instead on the right side of my mouth on an aching tooth. I kept my hand pressed against my cheek to quell the ache. I had popped a pain killer just before leaving the house, but even though I had easily crushed the tablet between my thumb and forefinger – few people have the strength to be able to do that by the way – thrown the powder into a glass of hot water that Ma handed me, stirred the contents with a spoon and swallowed, the medicine had yet to react. Another fifteen minutes or so and hopefully the pain would subside. At that moment though while I was waiting for the bus I had a throbbing toothache and that's what brought me to her attention.

'Are you in pain?' she said, frowning in concern. 'Do you need a medicine? I have one.' And she made as if to open her bag and take out the medicine, till she saw me shake my hand to indicate that I didn't need a pill.

'It's nothing,' I said. 'Becoming wise is never easy.' And I let out a world-weary sigh.

'Wisdom tooth then?' Her frown gave way to a lovely sparkle of teeth. The most beautiful, innocent smile I had ever seen.

I enjoy making ambiguous statements now and again, to prompt people to ask me what I meant, and I expected a probing question from her, not an intelligent guess.

'Well done,' I acknowledged.

'Not for me.'

'Do you always figure things out?'

'No,' she smiled again. 'It's because both my parents are dentists.'

The analgesic was now working and the pain already considerably less but to elicit the warmth of her sympathy once more, I let out an 'Ah...my god!'

'That bad?' The frown of concern was back. 'We can go to my father's clinic right now. He'll help ease the pain.'

'No, don't worry.' I removed my hand quickly. 'It's better already. That was just a temporary twinge. The pain killer seems to be working.'

'That is good to hear but do visit Dad's clinic. He's a very good dentist. He's even written a book on how to take care of your teeth. Mom's also very good. Oh, there's my bus!' A dark blue coloured bus came into view, the letters Bal Bharti School emblazoned all over it.

'I'll surely go,' I assured her. 'I do need to get my teeth looked at.'

'When you visit, stop by to say a hi to me too.' She held out her hand. 'I'm Ayushi. Ayushi Tandon. My dad's Dr Rajesh Tandon. You must have seen his board.'

'Rahul.'

I covered her soft fair hand with my own large brown one. Her hand was small and delicate, a quarter the size of my own paw. My hand is the size of a bear's paw with strength to match. I was careful not to squeeze her hand too hard. Ma keeps telling me that I am not aware of my own strength, and she's right.

The bus came to a halt. She quickly withdrew her hand. Even though I was already mesmerised, I believe that I would have dismissed her friendliness as simply good manners, had it not been for a few extra, small gestures that she made. Small things but they mattered. She looked into my eyes for those extra couple of seconds before hopping on to the bus. From her window seat she waved and said, 'See you soon!' and her eyes were locked with mine till the bus turned the corner.

This was good. She seemed keen to pursue a friendship with me, I thought. And if that was the case, I was frankly overjoyed at the prospect. I barely had a couple of friends in this neighbourhood. I hopped on to my bus that came ambling by and was lucky to get a seat for the hour-long journey to college. I couldn't get Ayushi out of my mind. Her child-like genuine concern made me smile.

As the bus trundled away I felt my life had changed forever. Was she the 'smart' girl my father had spoken of who would see through appearances? I started to fantasise. With monumental effort I brought myself to earth and did a quick reality check. May be I was reading too much into that five-minute encounter. But what was also true that not many girls had shown too much interest in me. Anyhow, I decided there and then to cancel my scheduled appointment with my regular dentist. Dr Gupta, at the University Hospital Services, and fix one to go and see Ayushi's father, Dr Tandon instead.

* * *

It was on a Friday that we had met. Friday the 13th of May 2008 to be precise. It was so hot already air-conditioners in most flats were running 24/7. Despite the oppressive heat there was a spring in my step that had been absent hitherto. Even my dear mother who is not the most observant person on the planet noticed my uplifted spirits.

'Is it a girl, Rahul?' she asked without any preliminaries, just the way all mothers do.

'What? Of course not, Ma,' I denied vehemently. 'Where do I have the time?'

'Something is going on, I can sense it,' she said.

You may find it astonishing how quickly and hard I had fallen for Ayushi, but the reason why no girl had shown much interest in me ever before had to do with the way I look: big nose, big ears and thick lips. Over-weight would not properly describe my body, because most over-weight people are podgy. Compared to the over-weight boys in college I may have been even bigger in girth, but unlike your regular coke guzzling kid, I was muscled all over.

Years ago, my father encouraged me to go to the gym. I had been over-weight since childhood and he said it would help me shed weight. The workouts did not remove even ten grams fat from my body, but what it did was convert my body fat into rock hard muscle that any *pehelwan* would be proud of.

Most people though are not aware of my muscles till I remove my shirt and they step back in sheer surprise seeing my Mr Universe muscles. My strength has taken bullies in school and college by surprise. In the past sometimes when I was a fresher, and the local *dada* made the mistake of trying to bully me, all I did was remove my shirt and flex some muscle. Just a demo was enough. They very well see that I'm speaking from a position of strength they can only aspire to or dream of.

My father once jokingly suggested to my mother that they should send me to Japan.

'Why?' she had asked.

'He will be the first Indian Sumo wrestler to give the Japs a run for their money,' he laughed, pride evident in his voice.

How I miss Dad. He was a great father in so many ways, but the best thing about him was that he accepted me the way I was. I miss our table tennis sessions and his advice on life. My father was a table tennis enthusiast and had played for his college. He got me hooked to the game too hoping I would lose weight. I didn't but I started to move around the table and wield the bat faster than he could have ever imagined. The gym gave me muscles and strength but it was table tennis that gave me agility and razor sharp reflexes. Dad wanted to send me to Thailand to learn martial arts skills, and said it would be cheaper than Tokyo and closer to home. He passed away before that could ever happen and now it's just the two of us left: Ma and me.

I love my mother dearly, and she's all I have now. She has so many ailments that my Dad and I were constantly looking after her. Now it's all fallen on me. She has asthma, issues with her blood pressure and trouble with her kidneys for which I need to take her to hospital whenever there is an aggravated situation. Ma also suffers from serious migraines that attack her frequently and has to lie down. She can be on her feet only for about six to eight hours; the rest of the time she's either sleeping or battling migraines. When Dad was around he took her to innumerable doctors but no one could help her. I mention this to make you understand that in many ways she is dependant on me now that Dad is no more.

One day, I remember Dad and I had a particularly gruelling marathon session of ten games of table tennis when he said something to me that I'll never forget.

'I need to tell you something important,' he said when we went out into the lawn, and sat down on the garden chairs to catch some of the cool evening air that would dry out our perspiration. We had been allotted an old, British style small bungalow in the university, adjacent to the college where he taught.

I thought it would be something about my game or about studies but what he said took me by surprise.

'Rahul, you're now at an age where you'll find yourself attracted to girls.' He leaned back and lit his pipe. 'So, are you? Anyone you like?'

'Well....' I stammered.

'It's natural if you are getting attracted to them.'

'Yes, Dad, I am, yes.'

'Okay, good.' He tapped at his pipe gently, a habit whenever he chose his words carefully. 'Now what I'm going to say might sound hurtful but I'm going to say it anyhow.'

I waited.

'This is what I want to say.' He drew on his pipe. 'You will find girls attractive, but...' he paused, '... you may not always find them responsive to you.'

I wondered if he had been reading my diary. At the time there was a girl in class, Nitya, a tall, dark South Indian girl, on whom I had a crush, but she was clearly not interested. I started to suffer from low self-esteem.

'Don't get me wrong,' he said. 'They will be happy to be your friends but they might not like to be your girlfriends. Do you know why?'

I was embarrassed and hurt. Of course I knew. I wasn't stupid. Did he have to rub it in though?

'It's because I'm fat,' I said in a sullen tone. 'But there's nothing I can do. We've tried...'

'Stop right there,' he said. 'And listen carefully to what I have to say. Girls may not find you attractive but let me tell you not as your father but as someone speaking objectively they are being foolish. Not wanting to go out with a fat boy I can understand – although that too is debatable – but you, you are not really fat. You are a very strong boy with a great heart and brain. Do you understand what I am saying?'

I nodded. *What was his point?*

'My point is this,' he said, reading my mind. 'Never feel inferior if girls don't show any romantic interest in you. They don't know any better. If you were in Japan, my son, all the girls would want you there because they would understand soon enough that you're not just a fat boy who eats too much and has no stamina. You are a very athletic and healthy boy full of energy. So, if Indian girls don't know any better, don't worry about it.' He leaned back and laughed uproariously. 'When you grow up we'll find you a *geisha* in Japan. You know who that is?'

'Sort of.'

'Not only *geishas*, the regular Japanese girls will like to be close to you.' He paused. 'Even some Indian girls will think of you the same way, but they will have to be the smart ones who can see who you really are. In the meanwhile, my son, don't take any rejections to heart.' He stood up. 'Come let's get in one more game. I need to beat you again.'

Self-esteem restored, I followed Dad into the garage to resume our battle.

* * *

I turned up at Dr Tandon's clinic, literally a stone's throw away the very next day, a Saturday. I had seen the signboard even before I had met Ayushi so I knew where the clinic was. A young, dark woman wearing a white uniform met me as soon as I entered. After consulting quickly with the doctor who was in surgery, she said he would see me as I was in pain, but the next time would have to be with an appointment.

It was a garage that had been converted into a dental clinic. The lady, who wore a dark shade of lipstick, manned a very small reception area beyond which lay two cabins, one for Dr Tandon and one for his wife.

'Dr Tandon doesn't have too many patients today,' the woman said in Hindi. 'You come after forty-five minutes.' She looked at me with sympathy as she saw me pressing my cheek hard with my hand.

An hour later when I returned, I was shown into Dr Tandon's cabin. He was a bespectacled, middle-sized man with a French beard. He motioned for me to sit on the dentist's chair.

'I don't think this is a case of extraction,' he said, after giving my mouth a careful examination. 'Your wisdom tooth can be saved. So let me just give you a temporary filling today. Okay?'

I nodded and he proceeded with his work, making polite, general conversation all the while describing the condition of my teeth and advising me on how to take care. He also periodically gave out instructions to a young Nepali boy, not much older than me, who assisted him in his work. I gathered that Shiva – the assistant – managed the doctors' appointments, assisted in surgeries, and also doubled up as a compounder dispensing medicines as per the prescriptions.

What struck me about Dr Tandon was how, while speaking to me, he combined politeness with matter-of-factness in his tone as well as in his words, which inspired confidence in me about his abilities.

'Okay,' he said eventually. 'We're done. Come back after a week.' He paused. 'Where do you stay?'

'Just near Dr Mukul Sharma's clinic, sir. The flat opposite his.'

'Oh, I see,' he said. 'Dr Sharma is a good friend of mine.' He scratched his head. 'I know where you stay. I think Dr Sharma treats your mother, isn't that right?'

I nodded.

'I've met your mother once,' he said. 'A fine lady.'

He now knew my bearings and would be able to trust me.

This was the moment.

'Sir,' I said. 'I wanted to see Ayushi. May I? Will she be at home?'

He looked at me carefully and didn't seem to dislike what he saw.

'Are you with her in school?'

'No, Sir, I'm in first year, college. I met her at the bus stop. It was she who suggested I see you for my tooth.'

'Oh, she did, did she?' he laughed. 'Well, she did the right thing then.' He glanced at his watch. 'Yes, she should be at home at this time. You know the next block of apartments? Our flat is two floors up. Just ring the bell.'

* * *

I left the clinic euphoric. I had got the father's permission to visit his daughter. None of the hurdles or cross-examining I had worried about.

I rang the bell and a surly faced Nepali who examined me with suspicion opened the door. When I explained that I had come to see Ayushi, his suspicions seemed to increase not lessen. Fortunately, Ayushi rescued me by appearing just then and gave me one of her warmest smiles.

'Come on in! You remembered to come and see me,' she said. 'Are you just coming from the clinic?'

I nodded.

'Great! Come to my room.' She turned to the man. 'Hetram*ji*, two Cokes, please. Okay for you?'

I nodded.

The man called Hetram said: '*Ji*, Baby.'

The manservant's face was impassive when he brought us our drinks, but I suspected that he still didn't approve of me. Maybe he thought I was too old to be Baby's friend.

We made small talk. I asked about her plans after school. She didn't have a plan as such, but wanted to be famous. I spoke about my last year in school and how I hadn't done as well as I had hoped. She said she was struggling with maths. Stuff like that.

When I went home that day I was happier than I had been in a long time.

* * *

Schools were closing for a two-week mid-term break and I thought I wouldn't see Ayushi in the mornings anymore. To my surprise, a few days later I found her waiting at the bus stop at exactly the same time. She wasn't in her uniform but in a light blue tracksuit that had her school logo imprinted. And a pair of orange Nikes.

'I thought school was shut for a break,' I said.

'It is,' she responded, 'but some of us are in training for a big inter-school sports event next month.'

'So you're into sports, then?'

'Kind of.' She smiled, showing her pearly white teeth.

'What do you play?'

'Table-tennis.'

I stared at her momentarily speechless. Not only was smart, she also played table tennis! This was truly a sign from the heavens above.

'So whom do you train with?' I asked.

'The captain of the boys team, but he's not that good. Most of the time he struggles to beat me. And sometimes I beat him.'

'I could train you,' I offered.

She started to laugh, but quickly covered her mouth with both her hands and stopped herself. I guess she didn't think I was much of a player, but only sort of hitting on her.

'It's really nice of you to offer, but I play really well. ... We can play once the tournament is over. Meanwhile I need to practice really hard with the best players. I hear some of the other schools have really great teams.' Her bus came in view just then. 'Okay, I better rush. See you.' And with a swift wave she was off.

I let out a long sigh. What was I thinking? It was an impossible idea to begin with. I shouldn't even have asked her and made a fool of myself. I should be content with what I had, which was this ten-fifteen minutes of conversation with her each morning. Now that I knew she was going to school every day, I made sure I took my bus at the same time. It didn't matter that sometimes my classes began much later. And it also didn't matter that on Mondays and Fridays they began sooner. For her sake, or rather for those ten minutes of conversation or of being with her really, since sometimes we were mostly silent, I was missing an important class.

My mother noticed I wasn't leaving as early as usual on those days. I made an excuse, just as I did at university. 'It's my mom,' I explained to the professor. 'She's not been keeping well, so I need to handle some chores in the morning...' Of course I felt guilty about telling lies to Ma and at university, but what could I do? I couldn't lose a chance to spend time with Ayushi.

One morning at the bus stop I found Ayushi despondent, not her usual bright self.

'Anything the matter?' I said.

'That boy you know, the one I was training with...He's come down with a fever and isn't coming to school anymore. And the rest? They play so badly that I could give each one of them under ten. So now I don't have anyone good to train with.' She scratched her chin. 'I'm not even sure if it's worth going to school for training any more. I mean – what's the point? It might improve *their* game, but it might actually bring mine down.'

'Well, I ....' The words were out of my mouth before I could stop myself.

She stared at me. 'Yes, I'm sure even you will be better than the other players.' I winced when I heard her say 'even you' but I let it pass. This was the girl I loved. Yes, loved.

'But what about your classes?' she asked. 'You can't miss them, can you?' That was said in a way as if it was the end of the world, little realising that I was already missing one for the sake of the small bit of conversation we were having.

'No classes today,' I lied. 'I was just going to the univ to meet some pals. I can always meet them some other time. But how will I enter your school?'

Just then her bus turned the corner and made its way towards us.

'Come on,' she said, as she climbed the first step. 'Don't worry. No one will ask because none of us are wearing uniforms today.'

I followed her down the aisle of the mostly empty bus.

'Besides,' she turned to give a sly wink, 'I know the *chowkidar*. If he asks any questions, I'll say you're my cousin. Don't worry.'

The bus sped on. It was a bright, sunny day.

* * *

The first game she nearly beat me. To be fair to myself, I hadn't played in a while. It takes time to get used to the speed of a table and I didn't have my regular racquet. The one provided to me was a lacklustre wooden affair with a pasting of rubber on it the width of an eggshell. Ayushi herself was using a Butterfly, an upper-end model she had saved up for over several months of her pocket money. When we drew level at 19/19, I decided to use one of my special serves. Two special serves for which there was no come back. Game.

She had been gaping at me with increasing astonishment throughout the game. Now her mouth fell wide open with disbelief.

'Rahul!!' she practically screamed. 'You're amazing! My goodness, I could never have *dreamed* that you could play this well. You beat me. Me! The captain of the girls' team.'

Legs evenly spread apart and crouching over the table she assumed a determined and serious stance for the second game. Poor Ayushi. She wanted to get revenge for having lost the first game. She didn't stand a chance. By now I had rough familiarity with my racquet, and knew what it could and could not do. I also understood the 'speed' of the table as well as with her style of game, so it was an easy win for me. Under fifteen. She was laughing and crying at the same time at the ease with which I had beaten her.

We played another ten games, back to back. I won all of them easily even though I had decided not to play my best so she didn't feel too demoralised. Afterwards we went to the school canteen to grab a bite, which was kept open for those coming in to train.

'You play like a pro,' she said, in between munching a chicken sandwich.

'I guess you could call me semi-professional.' I explained how I had nearly made it to the Delhi state team. There were four players who were to be selected from a couple of hundred that were competing and I nearly made the grade. I was narrowly edged out, coming fifth. All the four who made the grade were much older boys; the coach was confident that I would make it to the state team the following year. At the time medical school entrance tests were coming up and Dad – falling under pressure from Mom's arguments — felt the game would distract me from my studies.

'Finally,' I said, ruefully, 'I didn't make it either to medical college or to the state team.'

'Shucks,' she said. 'That's a real shame.' She put her hand over mine in sympathy. It felt nice, soft and warm.

After lunch we went back to the gym. I taught her how to play rallies and at the same time move away from the table. Some of the other kids came to watch. She didn't know any spinning although she was great with her slices and chops. Her forehand smash was a killer. I stood behind her, held her hand and showed her the angle at which the racquet should hit the ball for a good topspin.

* * *

After that day she was the one to pester me to go to school with her. The following Saturday she called me early in the morning.

'Hey Rahul,' she said. 'Are you free today?

'Yeah,' I said, trying to sound casual.

'I was thinking, could we practice some more? School starts Monday with classes all day. I'll get time only in the evenings, but you probably won't be able to get in. They'll want to see you in the school uniform.'

I was quiet, thinking hard.

'I could get one tailored,' I nearly said, but stopped myself just in time. That was a lame suggestion. Besides even with a uniform – and where would I find the money to have one tailored – they would eventually figure out that I wasn't a student. I might even get Ayushi into trouble. It was a stupid idea and I only mention it to tell you how besotted I was with her.

'It'll be our last day of practice,' she pleaded mistaking my silence for reluctance. 'Say you'll come.'

'Sure.'

So we went to her school for the very last time and we played twenty games back to back.

'You know, Rahul,' she said, during lunch at the school canteen that day, 'you'll make a great husband for some girl one day.'

'You're kidding me.'

'I'm serious! Cross my heart and hope to die.'

I continued to maintain my 'don't-make-an-ass-of-me' expression.

'I am serious.' She looked at me with perfect sincerity. 'I mean, you're so smart and funny. Okay, you *look* fat and no girl likes fat, including me, but you're *not* fat.' She leaned across and tried to pinch my shoulder. 'All muscle there.' She poured ketchup on her plate. 'To be honest, now that I think about it, it's really stupid to judge people like this.'

That day before lunch it had become so hot inside the gym that I asked if I could remove my shirt. It was game fifteen of the day and I had been jumping about a lot. My fault. I had taught her how to place the ball so that you kept your opponent on the move not even giving him time to breathe.

When she nodded, expressing surprise that I had even asked, I took of my cotton shirt, which was drenched in sweat. Of course once I remove my shirt everyone realises that I am not simply a fat, pulpy boy.

'Wow!' she said. 'Rahul!! Your physique is quite something.'

'Ah, no.' I tried to make light of it.

'Do you exercise a lot?' she said.

'Two hours every morning.'

'You should be in films,' she said. 'You'd be the real hero.'

I blushed at the attention she was giving me.

'You have shoulders like the Mongolian,' Dad used to say, referring to a Mongolian Sumo wrestler who had bested most of the Japanese champions.

After the game was over she came over to me and caressed my back gently – I was still wearing a vest. 'You're a strong guy, Rahul.'

I nearly said something foolish about how much I loved her but stopped myself in time.

* * *

Everything went well between the two of us till the day a couple of Ayushi's friends joined us at the bus stop. A lean, pimply boy named Sudhir and a yet thinner, dark girl called Shobha. They boarded the bus one stop ahead previously but as roadwork was going in area that bus stop did not exist anymore. As a result they now walked half a mile longer to reach this one, what I had by now begun to consider *our* bus stop.

Two is company, three is a crowd and four is way over-crowded. I couldn't enjoy the conversations I used to have earlier with Ayushi, which were sometimes fairly personal. Shobha clearly considered herself closer to Ayushi having known her for much longer. I hazarded that Ayushi too missed our chats but didn't know what to do. She couldn't very well stop talking to Shobha. What made matters worse was that Shobha went on and on about school gossip and the latest fashion trends, effectively excluding me altogether. Even when I went to Ayushi's apartment to meet her, to my great disappointment on several occasions they were both already there. Sudhir was like Shobha's shadow. Wherever she went, he followed.

'Let's go up to the terrace,' Ayushi suggested to me one day when the two were not there in her house. 'Nobody will disturb us then.'

The Tandons had their clinic on the second floor so the terrace was technically meant for their use. It was kept mostly locked but Ayushi had a set of the keys. So we went upstairs that day armed with a jute mat and a couple of cushions. We sat there, enjoyed the sun and chatted for a long time.

Over time this became a routine with us. She took pictures of us together with the new Samsung her father had given her for her birthday. And she put it on silent so that we weren't bothered by calls from Shobha or anyone else.

We started to have private meetings once again. She had sensed that I felt excluded. And I realised that she too enjoyed being with me.

I loved the talks Ayushi and I had. She told me that she liked the fine arts and wished to be an artist when she grew up. Her father, however, wished for her to be a doctor like himself, and had an entire library ready for her use. On my part, I shared my inner most thoughts with her, explaining how difficult it had been for me to come to terms with Dad's passing away.

Shobha clearly disliked me. I suspect she thought that since I was at university I shouldn't be hanging around with school kids, even though they were all going to finish school soon enough. She constantly sent me signals I wasn't wanted by cutting me off mid-conversation or not acknowledging me. *Who wants to spend time with you? It's Ayushi I can't bear to be away from.*

Matters came to a head one weekend at a McDonald's in a nearby mall. Ma had a migraine and so I decided to eat out. By the time I finished an important class assignment and reached McDonald's – Ayushi texted me to come – I was ravenous. I ordered a large burger for and a Diet Coke. I finished the burger in two minutes. It wasn't enough, I decided, so I went to get another one.

'Go easy, fatty,' said Shobha, as I was munching my way through the second one.

'It's probably his lunch,' Ayushi defended me. 'He's not a big eater.'

'This is post-lunch.' Shobha turned to me with a smirk on her face. 'He's already eaten a big meal for lunch. Haven't you, fatty?'

It was the first time she had called me 'fatty'. If anyone had called me that at college I would have coolly remove my shirt and flexed an arm. If they still wouldn't get the message I'd give them a bit of a bear hug. All done in a very friendly manner, but I would make it clear that I wasn't a podgy, pulpy pushover.

But this situation was different. Shobha was a girl. Also, I didn't want to leave a bad impression on Ayushi. So I hit back verbally.

'It's better than looking like some emaciated creature,' I said carefully casual even as I finished the second burger. 'Ah, that was good.' And so saying, I deliberately pushed the empty plate towards her.

Shobha reacted strongly. 'How dare you! Take that back!'

'Oh, you mean this.' Chuckling, I brought the plate back towards me.

'No, your mean comment. Apologise right now!'

'You take "fatty" back,' I said evenly.

'I said that for your own good so that you don't swell up like a balloon.'

'Or, like a pregnant woman,' giggled Sudhir.

So far it was harmless banter, but then things took an ugly turn.

'Do you like pork?' asked Shobha, her evil eye glinting again.

'Suppose I do,' I said.

'I thought so,' she said triumphantly. 'I think you should look for a pig as your girlfriend.'

To my surprise and increasing sense of humiliation everyone went into peals of laughter at her remark. Even Ayushi.

'Yes,' said Shobha. 'You should first have a pig as your girlfriend – and then later marry it.'

More laughter. The thing that hurt me the most was that Ayushi, instead of coming to my defence, was joining in the general mirth.

Shobha said, in between giggles, 'You'd better be careful. You're so fat you might be too heavy even for a pig.'

I stood up. 'I've had enough.'

'Oh, now you look like a red-faced pig,' said Shobha.

More laughter.

If I had stayed a minute longer I knew I'd reach out and wring that bitch's neck, so I stood up, turned around and walked off. I was in a massive rage. I knew I had to teach them all a lesson.

'Fat pig,' Shobha jeered loudly, even as I was walking away. Laughter.

I turned then, came back to the table and stared her down. One more squeak out of her and I would have grabbed her neck. She quietened down at once when she saw my expression, as I knew she would. Like all cowards. My can of coke was still on the table. I put my hand around it, crushed it, and shoved it inside Sudhir's shirt. I did this in a gentle, calm manner, but there was clear menace in my eyes. Sudhir started to shake and mumble apologies. Shobha looked like she was in shock. Cowards! They had never seen me like this.

As I walked away leaving the now silent trio behind, I was not only seething with anger but also broken inside. Not for what the others had said. I had enough of a thick skin but with Ayushi it had been different. Is this all that our friendship had meant for her?

* * *

As the saying goes hell hath no fury like a woman scorned. A supplementary should have been added: the fury of an ugly, fat boy who has been humiliated in the presence of the girl he loves is comparable. I'll show them, I kept on repeating in my mind. Shobha and Sudhir's barbs and laughter silence did not bother me; what had devastated me was that Ayushi had joined them in their laughter – it had hit me like an emotional sledgehammer.

I needed revenge. But how? I lay on my bed ignoring Ma's requests to come and eat dinner, just thinking of what I could do. I still couldn't think of harming Ayushi; my feelings of love for her were just too strong even if I did now hate her a bit as well. She had been under peer pressure I consoled myself. What could I do to the other two? I thought that I could grab Sudhir's arm the next time I saw him and twist it, not too badly but roughly enough to make him aware of my strength and scare the shit out of him. And add that I would break it the next time if he dared to humiliate me. Would that work? Or did I need to do something else? Something terrible to Shobha perhaps?

After dinner, I was still plotting revenge and thinking terrible thoughts when my telephone pinged.

'Sorry.' It was an SMS from an unknown number, but beneath the one word message was the name: Ayushi.

The next message made the mystery about the number clear.

'SIM not working. Using an old SIM instead.'

Did she think a simple sorry would fix it? I quickly deleted the message..

Five minutes later my phone pinged again. 'I'm really, really sorry.' Again, my rage did not abate. Did she think that a mere apology would sort it out? I knew Sudhir and Shobha would squeal to Ayushi if I tried any strong-arm tactics on them and I would fall in her eyes. Damn.

Ping, Ping. Two more messages.

'Sorreeee. Please forgive me. '

'Pleeease. I'll never forgive myself if you don't!'

What the hell was that? Did she really mean that? Or was she making fun of me? Were Shobha and Sudhir sitting over her shoulder as she typed her messages?

I scrolled down to the next one.

'Can you come over? I want to apologise.'

My doubts lessened. I looked at my watch. Just after midnight.

I SMSed back. 'Isn't it too late?'

'Never late for you. Please come. I need to see you badly.'

'Ok,' I responded, the spring back in my step. Ma was watching a late night serial. I waved aside her protestations about it being too late to go and see a friend.

'Something urgent, Ma!' I said. 'I'll be back soon but don't wait up for me.'

Before I left the house, I picked up a black canvas bag that had Ayushi's birthday present. The previous day, from one of my sources at the National Stadium, I had managed to get a pair of Chinese rubbers used for padding onto wooden table tennis racquets. I knew Ayushi was using the wrong racquet for her game. I'd show this to her and tell her why it would work for her. I was sure she would appreciate the gift.

* * *

She was wearing the same grey t-shirt and blue jeans from while we were at McDonald's. I didn't have to ring the bell when I reached her apartment. She was standing outside the main door waiting for me, her face drawn and anxious. I guessed the time of night was such that she didn't want me ringing the doorbell. Her parents, she whispered to me, as I followed her inside, had had a long day and were already in bed. I tiptoed past the living room and entered her bedroom.

She saw at once that I was emotionally shaken and disturbed. I had been happy enough en route but once I was face to face with her the memories of the evening came back with great ferocity. I was hurting inside all over again. She sat me down on a reclining chair in her room, and she herself sat down on the bed just opposite. We were both quiet, troubled in our own fashion. And then she took my hand in her small fair soft hands and stroked it gently.

Lowering her eyes in silent apology, she said: 'I'm so sorry, Rahul. I feel ashamed.'

I was quiet, almost ready to cry.

'You're my friend, Rahul and I love you as you are,' she said. 'Big, powerful. You're not ugly for me.'

Her words should have cheered me up, but I began to cry instead.

'You've broken my heart,' I sobbed. She stood up from the bed, came to me and held my hand.

'How can I make it up to you?' she said.

'You don't have to,' I said.

'I want to. Please forgive me, sweetie.' By now I was smiling in between my tears. The softness and sadness in her voice was that of the Ayushi I knew and it was balm to my pain. But I was still in agony. I thought of Shobha's graphic visual that had me marrying a pig.

'I need to do something,' she said, her brow creased in thought, 'to make it up for you.' Her next words took me by surprise. 'I know what I'll do. I'll give you all the medical textbooks that Dad has bought for me. That way you can prepare for the premeds at home instead of always sitting in the library.'

'No, no,' I said. 'You don't have to do any such thing.'

'I want to,' she said. 'There are at least six thick books that you'll find really useful.'

'Such as?' My curiosity was awakened. Getting into medical school in India was a tough business.

'Let me see,' she said, trying to remember. 'I have *Atlas of Human Anatomy* by Frank Netter. Then I have Robbins *Pathology* which I'm told is a classic.'

'Really,' I said, impressed. 'That's a fifteen hundred page monster. You have it?'

'I do,' she said, 'and several others.'

'Where are they?' I said, looking around.

'In the storage cabinet above that cupboard,' she said, pointing toward it. 'I can't reach it, but if you help...'

'Shall we do this some other time,' I said, suddenly conscious of how late it was. If someone were to come in and see me with you...it's very late. Let's not forget that.'

'Not a chance,' she said. 'Mom and Dad are fast asleep, and the aircon in their room is so noisy they can't hear anything.'

'What about your servant?'

'Hetram?' she said. 'Don't worry. It's his day off. He generally goes for a late night show.'

I thought about it for a few seconds and decided there was nothing to worry about. It was not as if we were doing something improper. So I nodded. Those books could be very useful. They would be definitely beyond my budget to purchase.

'Shall I get a chair from the dining room?' I offered.

'No need,' she said. 'You're strong enough to hold me up, aren't you?' She smiled. 'Come, let's get them.'

She walked across to the cupboard. The wooden cabinet was really high up, even for me, however, I managed to just about reach out for one of the wooden panels and open it, which I did.

'Okay,' she said. 'Well done!' And she jumped and hung to the inner section of the closet. 'Now just hold my legs and push me up.'

This wasn't something difficult for me to do; she was so light to lift up. I held her legs firmly as she rummaged about for the books. Bit by bit, she started to dig them out and throw them on to the bed where they made a soft muffled landing.

It was Robbins' *Pathology,* that thick tome that caused all the trouble. She pulled the large book towards herself with one hand, lost her grip and the both of us went crashing down on to the floor. It was lucky for her that I fell first for I had the bones to withstand such punishment. She fell on top of me, and I broke her fall, but she still seemed to have suffered some injury, for she did not get up at once.

'Sorry,' she said, even as she lay on top of me. I waited for her to get up.

'I think I've sprained something,' she said. 'Just give me a minute. I'll just be up.'

I could have got up on my own, and lifted her in the process, but I waited for her not wanting to aggravate any injury she may have experienced. The seconds rushed past as she grunted with pain and made an effort to get up. On the ceiling I saw the shadow of a human form. Hell.

He must have entered very silently for I didn't hear the door being opened. Meanwhile, Ayushi finally managed to get off me with slow movements and hopped across to her bed. Still on the floor, I turned around and was taken aback to see Hetram standing there, a scowl on his face. I was taken aback by the fury I saw on the Nepali's face.

'*Harami*!' His face contorted in anger. 'Bastard.' In his hands he held a golf club.

He must have standing silently behind the bedroom door all the while Ayushi had laid on me. We had both been so fully focussed on helping her get onto her feet without aggravating any injury she may have experienced that we hadn't noticed anything.

'What were you doing with Baby?' he shouted. '*Harami*!' Bastard.

Clearly he imagined that I had been up to some mischief. As he pulled the golf club over his head to gain extra momentum and force for the ensuing strike, I reacted quickly. He hadn't anticipated the swiftness of my response for I was up from the floor in a trice and was ready to dodge the blow, even as he lowered his weapon towards me.

At the very same moment Ayushi gave a shout and rushed to stop Hetram but it was too late. The club hit her instead on her forehead just next to her left eyebrow. A large bruise instantly formed, and she fell back on the bed with a moan.

I needed to grab the golf stick from this crazy man before he did any more damage. As I walked towards him he rained blows with the club on my arms and shoulders. They did not cause me much harm or pain. Unlike poor Ayushi who lay unconscious, I was built to take such punishment. Finally I reached him. With one hand I easily wrested the golf club away from him. His body turned with the effort to retain his weapon. I bunched my other hand into a fist and smacked him hard on the back of his head. He fell like a log, and appeared to have passed out. I didn't think he would wake up soon.

I quickly turned my attention to Ayushi. How badly had she been hurt? Her eyes were shut and she had fallen silent after that first moan. The bruise had turned a dark ugly purple and was spreading. This wasn't looking good at all! I put my finger under her nose; she was alive. Phew. I needed to quickly go and wake up her parents so that she could get medical attention. I had decided to do just that when I heard another sound behind me.

I turned quickly. It was the Nepali again! Unbelievable. I had hit him so hard. Usually a man of his build would have been knocked out for at least an hour. His eyes were blood shot and his lips stretched in a snarl.

'*Abhi tu dekh*, now you watch,' he said, as he brandished the shiny curved object in his hand. It was a khukri. In the time I had been attending to Ayushi he must have taken it out from somewhere. I will never know how he got his hands on it so quickly. Perhaps he had been carrying it with him on his person all the while somewhere in reserve when he attacked me with the golf club.

From the look on his face I didn't doubt that he meant to kill me. He lunged forward and slashed at me with his weapon. I narrowly escaped these onslaughts. He slashed again. Once, twice, thrice. I had to do something immediately now that there was no barrier between the khukri and me.

Since I was much taller than he was, he rightly judged my stomach to be the best place for him to attack. He slashed once again with all his might. Steeling my nerves and moving at lighting speed – this was a matter of life and death – I caught his arm while it was still in motion as if it were a table tennis ball that I needed to connect with my racquet. He had a look of shock, wonderment and utter incomprehension. I easily wrested the weapon from his hand. The tables were now turned, but I had no plans of injuring him but only of explaining the situation.

'Hetram!' I shouted. 'Stay away. I mean you no harm.'

Scarcely listening to me, despite the khukri in my hand now, he lunged at me. What on earth was he thinking? The next moment I understood. He grabbed my testicles and started to squeeze. I was in agony and going to faint any moment.

I caught his arm and pushed him back. The next moment the pressure on my private parts vanished. He fell off balance and retreated a few feet. He quickly straightened up then and came at me again. In sheer desperation, I swung the khukri at him. It struck him on the neck and a trickle of blood appeared. I felt the khukri hit another object as it passed him.

Hetram's body hit the floor with a thud.

I turned back to Ayushi now and I froze. A large pool of blood was forming around her. I placed my finger under her nose. Her breath was gone. I felt for her pulse. Nothing. She was dead. My dear, beloved Ayushi was dead. And I had killed her.

A painful realisation dawned on me. I had sensed the khukri had connected with another object after inflicting an injury on Hetram's neck. That object had not been an object. It had been her. The sharp edge of the khukri, still swinging after having wounded Hetram, had sliced off her carotid artery. She had instantly started to bleed to death. Could I have possibly saved her if I had woken up the Tandons and we had attended to her at once? That's a question to which I will never know the answer.

* * *

I sat on the floor next to Ayushi's dead body, my face buried in between my knees, sobbing hysterically. I didn't dare lift my head and open my eyes. After what seemed an interminably long time I turned to look at the clock on the wall and realised it was past three o'clock in the morning. I started to think about what I should do. I could hammer on Ayushi's parents' bedroom door and wake them up.

But what would I say to them? 'I have accidentally killed your daughter – please forgive me.' They would probably kill me with their bare hands. It was a foregone conclusion that not a word of what I would say would be convincing enough for them. Or even the bare fact that it was at her instance I had come over? It was no wonder that the Nepali didn't listen to what Ayushi was trying to shout out in my defence. He could not understand that she was lying in that intimate position with me by sheer accident. In any event Hetram was a loyal servant and probably thought he needed to give me a beating at the very least. And then everything spiralled out of control.

* * *

Not the Tandons. Not the police. Not anyone. No one would ever believe me. No one. The police would immediately arrest me for both the murders. Shobha and Sudhir would testify against me. They would say it was a revenge killing because of the minor altercation of the previous evening. And they wouldn't have been framing me; all concerned would genuinely believe that. To be fair, the idea of revenge had crossed my mind, even if it had been momentary, but Ayushi had not been the target.

What would happen to my dear mother? It was that thought that troubled me now. I was her only anchor. Her only support. She would be destroyed. To first lose her husband prematurely and then have her son arrested on charges of a double murder. She might even end her life. No, I couldn't allow that to happen. After losing Ayushi, lose my mother. The very idea was unbearable. I began to sob again, but now I knew that daylight was not far and I needed to do something.

I couldn't hold my mind still enough to think. I then remembered that when I had entered Ayushi's bedroom on the way through the living room, we had passed by a dining table on which was lying a bottle of Ballantine Scotch. I stood up, went out into the semi-darkness and brought in the bottle. It was half full. I took a good gulp, a second one, and a third one. It burned my throat as I gulped it, but it helped to calm me down and straighten out my thinking.

I understood two things once my nerves calmed. Firstly, that it was a very bad idea to wake Ayushi's parents and tell them what had transpired. Secondly, I had to act fast. I couldn't risk them waking up for some reason, and coming in, to see how their daughter was doing. Ayushi had told me that they never came out of their bedroom at night. Still, it was a possibility that could not be ruled out. Besides it would soon be daylight.

First things first. I had to get rid of Hetram's body. If I left the house with both dead bodies inside the room it would be clear to the police that it was the work of an intruder. With no signs of forced entry, they would immediately think of Ayushi's friends, among other possible suspects. It would only be a matter of time before I came under their radar. Once Shobha and Sudhir were questioned by the police as they were bound to be, they would talk of the demonstration of my physical strength and the threatening posture I had adopted the previous evening at McDonald's.

Once the police had me in their custody, I knew that they had their own foul ways of extracting information. My physical strength would not matter a whit when pitted against a police familiar with the use of torture to extract confessions.

If I somehow managed to get rid of Hetram's body, at least temporarily suspicion would fall on him. In the morning the parents would find only Ayushi's dead body and Hetram missing so they would conclude that it was Hetram who had killed their daughter. They might even think he had been drinking the Scotch. I took another deep gulp from the bottle. That was right. My thoughts were clearing. The thing to do was to somehow get rid of Hetram's body.

I could easily carry the servant's body, he was of a light build, but where could I dump it? In the gutter that ran outside the colony? A bad idea. That drain was too shallow and the body would be quickly discovered. I could be spotted by one of the watchman who walked about banging their sticks. Besides all six gates to the locality were closed at this time of the night, barring one that was manned by a security guard. No, I couldn't carry Hetram very far.

It came to me then. I needed to dump the servant's body on the terrace for the time being. Later, I could think of how to get rid of it. The terrace was locked, but Ayushi had the keys. I rummaged in the pockets of her jeans and found a bunch of keys inside. I recognised the one used for the terrace; we had been upstairs quite a few times.

Before I took care of Hetram's body I needed to do a few things. I had to take Ayushi's phone with the SIM since it would have a record of messages sent to me. I also decided to tidy up the room so that if by any chance the parents decided to check on Ayushi they would not notice the blood but only see the room was in order and the outline of her daughter sleeping peacefully. I covered Ayushi with the flannel blanket that lay next to her.

I went towards Hetram's body that lay on the floor in a pool of blood. It occurred to me that if someone saw blood on the stairs his body would be discovered at once. I needed to make sure that there was no blood there. I quickly found a large white bed sheet inside Ayushi's cupboard, spread it on the floor, picked up the dead man's body and placed it on top.

I left Hetram's body wrapped inside the bed sheet, and then went to where Ayushi lay on the bed. Her pillow had already soaked up the blood and turned red, as had the bed sheet. I felt terrible leaving her like this but there was nothing I could do. I was helpless.

And then I kissed her hand, and asked her to forgive me. It was all one terrible and ghastly accident.

I wiped my tears and hurriedly grabbed her Samsung, threw it inside my bag, which I then hoisted on my shoulder. I switched on her bathroom light, and switched off the bedroom light so that it would remain in semi-darkness, and the blood not be noticed by one of the parents, should either of them wake up. The bed sheet had been straightened, and her stuff was in its usual position.

With my hands now free I placed them underneath Hetram's legs and waist, picked up the body wrapped in the bed sheet and slowly and silently made my way out of the house trying to make sure that I didn't collide with any piece of furniture on the way. Moonlight came in through the window helping me find my way out of the flat without knocking anything over. Opening the door while carrying Hetram might have proved difficult for anyone else, but I managed it without too much difficulty. I deliberately didn't close the outside door just in case I needed to come back in. Outside the flat, there was far greater visibility since one of the staircase lights was already burning.

In deathly silence I made my way upstairs till I finally reached the terrace. I placed Hetram's body on the floor momentarily, unlocked the door, placed the dead man's body on my shoulders once again, and looked carefully for a place to hide the body. The longer the body remained undiscovered the better chances I had of not being suspected to have had anything to do with Ayushi's death. I dumped it in a corner, but when I turned to leave I saw that there would be clear visibility from the adjacent terrace. I needed to prevent anyone who came up on the adjoining terrace from spotting the body. The body was wrapped up in a sheet but blood had soaked into the cotton fabric turning it red. Besides, even wrapped up, the outline of a human body was visible. This would not do. I dragged the dead man to a more suitable, less visible location. I caught sight of a large aluminium panel lying near the door that might have once been part of a cooler. I placed it on top of the Nepali's body partially obscuring it from view. There was one more thing I could do, I realised. If I hung up something up on the clothesline it would completely obscure the body. There was, by chance, a used bedcover lying on the terrace floor. I placed it back on the clothesline, and fastened it securely. Hetram's body was now hidden from view.

Now what? Did I have anything more to do in the apartment? Could I risk going in again? What for? Day was breaking even as I locked the terrace carefully and made my way down the stairs. I heard the sounds of people waking up. No, there was no way to go back in – and there was no reason to do so. Ayushi was dead. There was nothing I could now do for her. A final thought came to me then. Once Ayushi's body was discovered the first thing that the parents would do would be to call Hetram on his mobile. These days with advanced tracking systems, the police might be able to track the ringing phone to the terrace. The longer it took for the body to be discovered, the better it was. I searched in the dead man's pockets and found a mobile and a bunch of keys. I chucked both into my canvas bag.

My clothes were covered with blood, and I kept my canvas bag stuck to my chest to hide the stains. Thankfully no one spotted me; only a couple of stray dogs were sniffing around the trees. For the first time I was grateful for the poor street lighting in the area. It was still too early for anyone to be up and about. The voices I had heard were people just about stirring and waking up to an early morning.

Ma too was asleep when I got home. As soon as I entered the flat with my key I went to my bathroom and switched on the geyser. It was a warm morning, but I was shivering. I bolted my bedroom door from inside and stripped down completely. Even my undergarments were stained with blood. I put all my blood soaked clothes inside a blue Westside carry bag, put that and the other one with Ayushi's phone in it in my cupboard and then locked it. I would get rid of them later. I then had a long hot shower, put on a t-shirt and pyjamas and fell into a long, tired and dreamless sleep

* * *

I woke up hours later to the sound of someone banging on the door. My mind had temporarily blocked memories of the previous evening, so I opened the door expecting to see my mother. It was indeed Ma, but looked deeply concerned.

'Thank goodness, you're okay,' she said. 'Your friend – the girl you always spoke about – something terrible has happened to her. Where were you last night?'

'I wasn't at her place,' I managed to mumble, stepping out of my room. There could be no escape now from all the gruesome memories that instantly flooded back. I thought I would faint, and held on to the dining table. 'What's happened?'

She pointed at the television screen. The news was all about Ayushi's killing. The time bleeping on the TV was eight.

'It's the servant who did it,' my mother said as she flicked channels.

Everywhere it was the same news. The sight of poor, innocent Ayushi's face on the television screen was more than I could bear. I stumbled forward, collapsed in a heap on the sofa. I began to wail, and sob hysterically. I sobbed and I sobbed and I sobbed. What had I done? Ma came and sat besides me. 'It's okay, my dear,' she said, stroking my head. 'It's okay. Be brave.' What could I tell her? What could I do? Nothing could change the course of the events of the previous night. Nothing could ever bring Ayushi back to me.

I went out of the apartment a bit later to get some fresh air and soothe my nerves. It wasn't such a good idea. Everywhere there were small groups of people huddled together. Outside the Tandons' residence the police had set up barricades. By the evening they issued a statement that the servant Hetram was the prime suspect. Although it was too early to say, a police officer interviewed by one of the channels stated that it was possible that the servant may have violated Ayushi, killed her subsequently and then escaped. They were, he said, exploring all angles.

* * *

The Delhi police botched up the investigation from start to finish. Initially it was Hetram who was the primary suspect. Two days later they discovered his dead body on the terrace. Obviously, he couldn't have killed Ayushi, climbed up to the terrace and then killed himself. So he was eliminated as a suspect. The needle of suspicion shifted to the Tandons. The new theory was that Dr Tandon had woken up and seen his daughter having sex with the servant. That sent him into a rage and he killed them both. His wife assisted him.

The Tandons did not remain suspects for long. Due to the high profile nature of the case and the great public interest in the affair, the case was transferred to the CBI. The CBI rubbished the claims of the local police that the Tandons had committed double murders and instead began to suspect Shiva, the compounder and another man who helped one of Dr Tandon's associates in his surgeries. That's the way it went for quite some time, until the CBI decided that those two were innocent and then it was back to the Tandons who once again became the principal suspects.

* * *

After the events of that terrible night, I couldn't bear the sight of blood anymore. Even the sight of a bruise would bring back a flood of horrific memories. I could no longer dissect cockroaches or rats without starting to shake and shiver. I started to hate lab work. At last I told Ma that I had given up the idea of becoming a doctor for good and had decided to pursue law.

'Do what you like, *beta*,' she said. 'It's your decision.'

I passed the law entrance tests and joined the five-year LL.B course at Delhi University. Some of my professors from Zoo Oh were disappointed and sorry to see me leave.

While I was pursuing law I started attending the trial regularly. I went everywhere from the magistrates court where the Tandons were first produced to the sessions court where they were tried. I even visited the Supreme Court where they filed interim appeals against the trial court decision, hiring the services of a top Supreme Court lawyer. One policeman who was part of the investigation team realised that I was there during all or most of the hearings, thought it odd, especially since I didn't wear any tag from the media, came across and questioned me during a hearing at the sessions court. When I showed him my student ID and explained that I was studying for my law exams and planning to be a lawyer, he gave a loud guffaw and all his suspicions evaporated.

I didn't want any innocents to suffer for my actions, and I kept hoping that everyone would be acquitted, and the case would eventually be declared to be an unsolved and unsolvable mystery. I was sure that if I made a clean breast of it, no one would believe that I could have killed Ayushi and Hetram accidentally. When people go to see an action flick they don't consider it surprising when during a fight sequence the hero kills two persons with a single stroke of his weapon. In real life they would not believe the truth that it took all of ten seconds for a khukri to travel in one single arc causing fatal neck injuries on two different people.

All the years that the trial against the Tandons kept going on, for finally they were the ones who were charge-sheeted, I kept hoping and praying that they would ultimately be acquitted. Yesterday that hope was belied. The Tandons were both convicted of double murder and sentenced to life imprisonment. Had I not studied law, I may have come forward at this stage and made my confession but now with all these court visits and my studies I got a fair idea of law as well as of the slow churning of the Indian legal system. With Ma's health taking a turn for the worse the past few days, I couldn't risk leaving her alone and uncared for.

* * *

Most of India, rather Indians and interested persons across the globe believe that it was Ayushi's parents who killed her. The truth is that they were both fast asleep when terrible things happened in their beloved daughter's bedroom. The truth is also that on that day no murders took place. Two deaths did take place and there was admittedly great violence but that's not the same thing as murder. There is a clear distinction under the law – as there ought to be between murder and say, an accidental causation of death. I should know. I've been studying to be a lawyer for nearly five years now and you will see me in a black gown and white collar very soon.

I've sometimes wondered why Hetram didn't wake up the Tandons when he saw me with Ayushi. That would have been the proper course of conduct for him as a servant instead of grabbing his master's golf stick and attacking me with it. It may be that he was convinced that I had violated Ayushi's honour or was planning to, but our posture, to my mind, would have suggested to a man of greater intelligence that there had been no violence on my part. Then why? The only guess I can make is that he simply could not imagine that Ayushi could ever be intimate with someone like me in that way, or rather perhaps in any way. He possibly saw himself not only as a servant of the house but also as Ayushi's guardian since her parents were so busy with their dental practice. A conservative man the way most Nepalese are, the *gurkha* fighting spirit may have been so imbedded in him that upon first seeing Ayushi lying on top of me, without considering that we were both of us fully clothed and this may have happened as the result of an accident, unthinkingly, he straightaway went into attack mode. He may have had a misplaced confidence that he would be able to overcome any resistance from me easily. He may have imagined that the sounds of him giving me a thrashing with the golf stick would wake up Ayushi's parents and bring them to the bedroom. Like so many others before him he had completely underestimated my physical agility and strength. If only he had woken up the Tandons first, the proper thing for him to have done under the circumstances, everything would have turned out so very differently that night.

* * *

The court gave many reasons why it found the Tandons guilty of the murder of their daughter and servant. The motive for the crime was that Dr Rajesh Tandon had come across his daughter in a sexually intimate position with the servant, flown into a rage and killed them both. Plausible enough as a motive, but there needed to be evidence to give credence to this or any other theory. Here, the court observed that there was no sign of forcible entry. True enough. It was Ayushi herself who let me in. It said no single person could have carried Hetram's body to the terrace. False. If the judge had seen me doing my workouts at the gym and lifting weights he wouldn't have entertained any doubts on that score. The judgement observed that no one else but Dr Tandon would have dared to consume whisky after committing such a dead. How ludicrous is that? If I hadn't consumed liquor I could never have been able to sufficiently compose myself, carry Hetram's body upstairs or even remember to take Ayushi's mobile with me and tidy up the room. The incisions on the neck, the judgement concluded, were committed with a surgical instrument.

I can never ever fully atone for what I have done, even if it was all an accident. I will, however, try and be the best defence counsel in India, a person who will keep the prosecution on its toes. The good thing is that I trained to be a doctor before I became a lawyer. One of the things I will do once I have established my practice is pro bono work to improve the state of forensic work in the country. I may have caused the death of two innocent people, the harassment and even torture of others such as Shiva the compounder, and also the prolonged incarceration of two innocent persons, the Tandons themselves, but I swear upon those innocent lives, I swear upon Ayushi above all, that I will save many more lives, not as a doctor now, although that was my original intention, but as a lawyer fighting for justice and the truth.

And if many years from now when the last appeal is finally heard and disposed off, the Supreme Court too convicts the Tandons of a double murder and confirms the trial court sentence – I pray every night that this will never happen – I will step forward and confess to the crime.

* * *

Analysis of the Story in the Context of the Aarushi and Hemraj Killings

Before I commence any analysis of the story and explain the reason why it is placed in the book at this juncture, I render a full and unqualified apology to anyone close to Aarushi, be it her parents or relatives or friends, who is offended by anything portrayed in this story which is a work of complete fiction. In my personal view there is nothing wrong in a friendship a young girl may have with a young boy, but understand that others may have a different view and ask for their consideration in this regard. In the story I have the girl named Ayushi falling on a visiting male friend, while pulling out a book from the cabinet above the cupboard in her bedroom only for the purpose of establishing a possible motive for the servant to assault her friend. It does not in any way imply that any such thing happened.

What then is the purpose behind such a story? The prosecution brought in the golf club and the dental scalpel to create a compelling visual of what they alleged had happened. The second part of this book created an alternative visual " that of the servants assaulting Aarushi, the theory that CBI Team One found more credible. The purpose behind writing and inserting this story is to create, in the mind of the reader, yet another, a third visual, which is important because it shows us that *a third scenario was also possible.* And once the reader understands that yes, it was possible that it was a third person who committed the killings, he also becomes open to the possibility that it could have not necessarily been a friend, but any other third person.

Soon after the story begins it becomes clear to any reader broadly familiar with the Aarushi case that some things have been changed while others have not. So the Talwars become Tandons, Aarushi becomes Ayushi and NOIDA becomes Mayur Vihar. On the other hand, this is a tragic piece of fiction involving two dentists and the murder of their teenage daughter and servant under circumstances that broadly correspond to those in the Aarushi case – the very circumstances that were used to convict the Talwars. The Tandons too get convicted using similar arguments in court. For instance, how could any outsider have entered the apartment, why would have any outsider bothered to tidy up the room, how could a single person have carried the servant's body up to the terrace and so and forth.

In the story the girl Ayushi is herself standing outside the door in order to let her friend inside. In Aarushi's case too, there is no problem in a third person entering the apartment if she knew that person. Aarushi's phone was found switched off in real life; in our story her SIM is defective and she has replaced it with an older, still functional SIM. The story also provides a solution to a problem that baffled the police and investigators. This was the discovery of a fingerprint on the bottle of Ballantine whiskey that could not be matched with the Talwars or any of the other suspects. Why? It could be argued that this was conceivably the case because the killer was an outsider. Our fictional story does not, however, answer a few questions, for instance, that if the servant's neck was incised in Aarushi's bedroom, why was it that not a single drop of his blood was found there?

The story is admittedly somewhat fantastical and even far-fetched, but truth is stranger than fiction. It may be stretching things a bit to have our narrator Rahul kill two persons with a single swing of the khukri, but if you look at the case made against the Talwars, that too is fairly implausible. The truth in the Aarushi case may be something yet stranger and one that we will never know.

For more than half its length our story has a relaxed, even semi-comedic style. It only goes to show how Aarushi too was so full of life, and to give the reader a sense of what her loss must have meant for her parents.

Is the story relevant to the case itself? Yes, it is because let us not forget the five golden rules that the Supreme Court laid down in the case of *Satya Narayan versus State* previously referred to[112]. Two of the five golden principles read as follows:

Principle Two

The facts so established should be consistent only with the hypothesis of the guilt of the accused, that is to say, they should not be explained on any other hypothesis except that the accused is guilty;

Principle Four

They should exclude every possible hypothesis except the one to be proved;

Principle Two of the Supreme Court clearly enunciates that there shall be no conviction made only on the basis of circumstantial evidence if there *is any other hypothesis that could be consistent with the very same circumstances.* Principle Four provides that every other possible hypothesis should be excluded.

The prosecution argued that it would not have been possible for one person to carry Hemraj's dead body upstairs to the terrace alone; what they should have said was that it would not be possible for a man with an average build, or someone with the build and age of Dr Rajesh Talwar. Although in our story the protagonist Rahul does manage to take the servant's body to the terrace single-handedly, the implausibility of this happening ordinarily is exposed, as is that of carrying a body wrapped in a bed sheet that is leaking blood. The story does not answer many questions, but neither, for that matter, does the theory that the Talwars were the killers.

Aside from the ruling by the Supreme Court that convictions should happen only if all equally plausible alternative hypotheses can be ruled out, there was another purpose behind introducing such a story in the text. Lawyers and judges are for the most part hard headed and practical men of the world, and this perhaps is how they should be because they are dealing with hard, cold facts much of the time in a hard, cold world. At the same time this very attitude sometimes limits their imagination and they cannot perceive alternative scenarios fitting the very same set of facts so easily. They often do not realise that life is full of improbable circumstances, and this 'failure of imagination' together with various other factors already discussed in this book was also responsible for the ultimate conviction of the Talwars.

The Talwars were not legally bound to answer the question that if it wasn't them, who else could it have been? And yet this is precisely what they were asked, though not in so many words. It was as if there was a limited choice the sentencing judge had given himself: either the Talwars were guilty or the associates of the servant Hemraj. All other possibilities had been excluded to the judge's satisfaction.

The story I have introduced – that of an outsider being responsible for the killings purports to destroy several myths about the case. Firstly, it is maintained by the judge that no outsider could have committed the crime. Why? Oh, because he could not have accessed the Talwar residence or even Aarushi's bedroom even assuming that he somehow managed to get past the entrance and enter the flat. The story demolishes this assumption by demonstrating that Aarushi herself could have let in an outsider. There was of course yet another route via the guest bathroom that linked up to Aarushi's bathroom and which opened up to her bedroom.

Whereas the scenarios discussed in the first two sections of the book deal with murders, the third scenario painted in the short story does not talk about two murders but two killings. All murders are killings but the reverse is not true. In choosing the title of this book *The Killing of Aarushi Talwar* I have left open the question whether or not it was a murder.

In this short story I have tried to destroy some of the so-called facts around the Aarushi murder. It is no doubt an extraordinary story about two extraordinary teenagers but it demonstrates for instance by creating a visual in the mind of the reader on how:

(a) An outsider could have gained access or rather been granted access by Aarushi herself.

(b) Instead of two murders, or one accidental killing and one murder, the case could have been one of two accidental killings. In the Aarushi case the investigating officer deposing on behalf of the prosecution stated in court that in his view Aarushi was accidentally killed by Dr Rajesh Talwar; a blow intended for the servant hit her by mistake.

(c) That it could have been possible for one person to have carried Hemraj's body to the roof

In his judgement Judge Shyam Lal carries on at some length about how Hemraj's associates or indeed any other third party could not have been the killers because there was a click shut lock installed in the door that led to Aarushi's bedroom. On the other hand the investigating officer of CBI Team Two is himself of the opinion that the door to her room was open.

Additional Superintendent of Police A.G.L. Kaul needed to say that the door was open for one very important reason. If that door wasn't open then it stands to reason that Rajesh Talwar would have knocked on the door to find out if all was well with Aarushi. If that door was shut, he could not have found Hemraj and Aarushi in a sexually compromising position. For the sake of argument, let's assume that Rajesh Talwar heard a noise from his daughter's room. How could he have known what was happening inside? He would have knocked, and even assuming that Hemraj and Aarushi were up to something, they would have quickly separated and no longer be caught in *flagrant delicto*, so to speak! The judge does not appear to have grasped the subtlety and sub-text behind A.G.L. Kaul's concession that the door to Aarushi's bedroom had been left open.

Since Aarushi's bedroom door had this click-lock feature, the judge avers, only she herself could have opened the door, unless someone had a key like her parents. Why on earth, the judge asks reasonably enough, would Aarushi have opened the door for someone she did not know?

This question of course assumes that the door was shut, which we do not know for certain. It may or may not have been shut when the parents went to sleep. It is also possible Aarushi came out for a drink of water or some such thing and then went back to her room, leaving the door ajar. It is even possible that she could have opened the door trustingly, without bothering to ask: 'Who is it?' There was no glass eye installed in the door through which she could have seen the face of the person knocking. There is no suggestion either that there was a keyhole through which he could have peered in.

There is another possibility this story explores. Aarushi could have opened the door to her room, and indeed the door to the flat itself for someone whom she knew. Someone could have rung the bell late at night; and Aarushi may have gone to open the door. Records show that in the evening her friend Sankalp called Aarushi several times on her mobile but it was switched off. He also tried her on the landline but no one answered it.[113] His last call was at midnight but the Talwars kept sleeping through the sound of the ringing telephone.[114] If they could not hear anything from the adjacent room due to the noise of the air-conditioner, they would in all probability have not been able to hear the doorbell either. There is no evidence that the split AC in Aarushi's room was noisy so *she* could have heard the doorbell ring and gone to answer it. In the story the girl Ayushi is already standing outside the apartment waiting to receive her friend Rahul so that he doesn't need to ring the doorbell. In real life it could have been the case that someone rang the doorbell, Aarushi went to attend it because Hemraj wasn't there and she saw someone whom she knew and therefore let into the house.

There was no evidence of 'forcible ingress and egress,' the judge writes in quaint old English that he uses on occasion. Yes, there was no evidence of forcible entry but that fact alone does not exclude all possibility of the killer being an outsider, for he could have been a friend or someone known to Aarushi who may have let him into the house.

It may well be argued that this story was unnecessary because there was simply no evidence of a stranger entering the Talwars' premises that night. This is factually not true. While there is no evidence of a forcible entry as Judge Shyam Lal notes, there is in fact evidence that a stranger *did* enter the Talwars' house that night.

The police found a bottle of Ballantine whiskey on the table. This had blood on it and also a fingerprint that could not be matched with anyone. Who was the person, this stranger who was never identified?

The prosecution argued that Dr Rajesh Talwar killed his daughter and the servant Hemraj and then hid the murder weapon, the so-called golf club. If Dr Rajesh Talwar were so clever and devious why would he hide the golf club and yet leave the whisky bottle on the table – which the police claim he kept drinking through the night to assuage his nerves after the double murder. His fingerprints were not discovered on that bottle. This is a matter of record.

The prosecution argues that Rajesh Talwar may have been drinking with gloves on. Would he be so clever and cautious so as to use gloves to drink whisky to soothe his nerves, and at the same time be so foolish as to leave bloodstains on the bottle? Those bloodstains had Aarushi's and Hemraj's DNA on it, but not Rajesh Talwar's. How could he possibly know that the blood would *not* have his DNA, but only the DNA of those who were killed that night, assuming that he was the killer?

Let us assume for a moment that he was drinking with gloves on (although this is extremely far fetched) but how did he *then plant someone else's fingerprints on the bottle?*

No answers here that either the investigators, prosecutors or the judge could provide. That important, but uncomfortable, question was simply, and conveniently, ignored. Fingerprints were discovered but they did not match any of the suspects.

The police did not match the bloodied palm print on the terrace, but even in all their carelessness they could not ignore a bloodied bottle of Scotch sitting on the table. What is very relevant is that the bottle had blood smears and both Aarushi and Hemraj's blood was found on the bottle, which gives rise to the fairly logical conclusion that the whiskey was being consumed by the killer *after* the murders. The blood of his victims on the killer's hands had been transferred on to the bottle. This was not all. There was a fingerprint. And this fingerprint was matched with all the suspects: the Talwars, Krishna, Rajkumar, etc. The print did not match anyone, and this crucial piece of evidence gives rise to the possibility that the murders/ killings that night were committed by a third party, a person possibly known to Aarushi.

Below are relevant extracts from the CBI's Closure Report:

> *DNA expert has confirmed the presence of blood of both the victims on a Ballantine scotch bottle which was seized from the dining table of Dr. Rajesh Talwar.*
>
> *There is no evidence to explain the finger prints on the scotch bottle (which were found along with blood stains of both the victims on the bottle). As per police diary, it was taken into possession on 16th morning itself. In spite of best efforts, the fingerprint could not be identified.*
>
> And finally:
>
> *The scientific examination results could not connect accused Rajesh Talwar with the crime and that in view of the above circumstances further judicial custody*

remand of accused Rajesh Talwar was not required in the interest of justice.

Someone Else Could Have Been The Killers

Our fictional story has a teenage girl's friend as the accidental killer. It is only an illustrative case. The killer could have been someone with a real motive for the killing and the deaths may not have been an accident. Who could possibly have a motive to kill an innocent fourteen-year-old girl? Unlikely, but it is possible that Hemraj was the main target for the killers, and Aarushi was collateral damage.

This is not something being pulled out of a hat, but a possibility that the police considered and eventually ruled out.

What is clear is Hemraj himself did fear for his life. There is the statement by Usha Thakur, a social activist who lived closeby that a fearful Hemraj contacted her barely *five days* before his murder.[115] This lady knew ex police officer K.K. Gautam, who spoke to the police about the depressed condition of the mattress on Hemraj's bed and the stinking toilet and gave testimony at the trial to this effect. With Gautam's assistance Usha Thakur gained entry into the flat and visited a guest bathroom that incidentally connected with Aarushi's bathroom that in turn led to her bedroom.

Hemraj, who feared for his life, had contacted Usha Thakur just days before his death. However, she had been busy and could not make time for Hemraj the day he contacted her. Their meeting was postponed and then the unfortunate incident occurred. He had wished to speak to her in private. It's a shame that Usha Thakur did not ascertain whom the threat came from, or that Hemraj would not tell her this on the phone.

Khumkala, Hemraj's wife also corroborated this real, or imagined, threat to Hemraj's life. Three years after the murders Hemraj's wife Khumkala came to India and said that the Talwars had been conspiring to kill Hemraj because he knew certain family secrets that they were concerned that he would divulge.[116]

This doesn't sound plausible. It is likely, to use the expression made famous by Judge Shyam Lal (this is how he described the maid, Bharti Mandal) that Hemraj's wife too being 'an illiterate and bucolic lady' misunderstood and misinterpreted what her husband was telling her. There is no explanation for why she took so long to appear. Her conviction that the Talwars conspired to murder Hemraj may have been influenced by reports in the Nepali press as well as sections of the Indian media (many Indian news channels are broadcast in Nepal) about how the Indian police was trying to falsely implicate innocent Nepali workers. Those who follow India's relations with her neighbours understand that there is an element of on-going tension with Nepal. Many Nepalis see India as a big and bullying big brother, and this perception sometimes gets translated justifiably, on other occasions unjustifiably into treatment of Nepalis in India.

Hemraj's wife's story about the Talwars gunning for her husband is not realistic for there was really nothing to stop Hemraj from leaving the employment of the Talwars if he feared for his life at their hands. Why would he continue to work with him *if he feared for his life*? It is far more likely that there was an external threat to his life.

Hemraj's wife's theory doesn't make sense but it is interesting because it shifts the focus and motive for the murders from Aarushi to Hemraj. In this view of the murders, Hemraj was the principal target and Aarushi was incidentally and accidentally killed. In other words it is exactly the reverse of the prosecution theory.

The question remains: whom did Hemraj fear? Why did Hemraj not clearly mention the Talwars if the threat came from them? It is more than likely that he did not name them because the threat did *not* come from them.

One possibility why he did not name the person(s) he feared was because it required him to provide some background or history as to why that person wished to cause him harm. The person's name, background and motivations had to be properly introduced. Had it been Rajesh Talwar he would have simply named him – or simpler still, packed his bags and left his employment.

The prosecution argued that Dr Rajesh Talwar attacked Hemraj whom he found in a compromising position with his daughter and hit his daughter accidentally.

A possible counter-theory is that on the night of the murders, a third party gained access to the Talwar residence where they had planned to kill Hemraj. Aarushi heard noises in the night, and stepped out of the room. The killers then turned their attention to her. She may have been accidentally killed.

Who Could Have Wanted To Kill Hemraj?

Who could this third party have been? There is at least one suspect whom the police did consider for some time but eventually let off. This was the Talwars' former servant, Vishnu Sharma (alias Vishnu Thapa), also a Nepali. He had been in the Talwars employment for ten years, much longer than Hemraj. Hemraj had in fact been brought in as a temporary substitute. The former servant was habitual of taking long holidays, and he would always leave a substitute during that period. On his return the substitute would leave.[117] In Hemraj's case the Talwars liked his work so much that they decided to keep him instead. The former servant, loyal for so long, must have been deeply upset at this turn of events. This was a betrayal by his employer, the Talwars, but much more so by Hemraj whom he had done a good turn by providing him with temporary employment and an income for a few months. It is likely that his anger would have been specially targeted at Hemraj who, in his view, turned out to be disloyal and one who had usurped his position in the Talwar household. He would have expected that out of his friendship, Hemraj would have turned down an offer of employment with the Talwars. The former servant could have borne with this development more easily had he been in service with the Talwars for a few years, but it was ten years, since the time Aarushi was only four. This was truly difficult to stomach, and it could have been a serious cause for taking 'revenge'. This possibility was explored by the police, as mentioned, but eventually discarded for the former servant was shown to be in Nepal at the time of the killings[118]. In other words, he had an alibi.

Stretching the bounds of possibility someone could say that the former servant had keys to the house and could have gained ingress. Knowing that the police would track him down, he decided to stay back in Nepal and may have assigned someone else this task. It may seem to be an outrageous suggestion – that a former servant could have hired someone else to make a hit – but stranger things have been known to happen. There are low-level assassins out there who carry out hits for ridiculously small sums of money. One of the curious developments in the Aarushi case the police could not explain was the eventual recovery of Hemraj's mobile phone in Punjab. The CBI mentioned this detail in their Closure Report. The police had been trying to track the phone ever since it disappeared. It surfaced in Punjab before it appeared anywhere else. This feeds into the theory of low-level and low-income professional killers. The Talwars would have ensured that they got rid of the phone had they been the killers. Rajkumar and Krishna the other suspects may have also thought it best to get rid of it; the stakes were too high for them. Some other low level assassin outside the radar of suspicion might have thought it worthwhile to turn a small profit and hand it over to an associate in another state.

Why did Hemraj not voice his fears to his employers, the Talwars, instead of to Usha Thakur, the social worker? It's possible he worried that if he shared his fears with the Talwars, they would either dismiss them as baseless or if it had any basis, decide to terminate his employment. After all, if such a mortal enemy existed the person would realise that the best place to kill him was inside the Talwar residence late at night, rather than down the street. Who was this enemy and what fierce hatred compelled him to execute Hemraj's murder and how did Aarushi become 'collateral damage,' if indeed this is what happened, is something we can only speculate about.

Part - Four

The Murder of Justice

'It's not a Justice System, it's just a system.' — Bob Enyart

THE MURDER OF JUSTICE: THE AARUSHI CASE AND OTHERS

Overview

Part One and Two of this book followed a certain narrative style. Each part started off with a proposition as to who the killers were, and then entered into a discussion as to whether the accusation could have been proved beyond reasonable doubt. In Part Three the story changes. There I attempted to show that a third person, an outside party could also have been the killer. This also incidentally feeds into the argument advanced in the first two segments that the Aarushi case was not one where the guilt of the Talwars or that of Hemraj's associates had been proved 'beyond reasonable doubt'.

The purpose of writing this book is not to find the killers, or even who the 'most likely' candidates were, but only to demonstrate that the killers may not have been properly identified, and the charges against them proved in a court of law beyond all reasonable doubt. This is the only proper way of dealing with the issue. The reader understands that an accused person cannot be convicted merely because it was possible, or plausible that he or she could have committed the crime. We are not even looking at 'likelihood' here. We are looking for proof 'beyond all reasonable doubt'.

As regards Part Two which projected the associates of Hemraj as the killers, a tangential but important argument made in favour of their innocence is that the police in this country are not particularly well-known for their kind disposition towards the underclasses, be they servants, rickshaw pullers or Nepalis with low paying jobs. Therefore, many would argue that the class divide in the country is such that had a shred of evidence actually existed against any of Hemraj's associates, the final CBI team (Team Two) that eventually prosecuted the Talwars would not have dropped the case against Rajkumar and Krishna. (Having said that a recent positive development is that action has finally started to be taken against those who oppress their servants, or exhibit behaviour tantamount to criminality towards their domestic help.[119])

The narco-tests allegedly implicated Hemraj's associates, but as the reader now understands there are good reasons why these are not admissible as evidence in criminal trials. Part of the weakness in these tests is that it is conceivable that an accused person may *imagine* making love to a woman; in the narco test he might say he actually *made* love to the woman although he never did. So also Rajkumar and Krishna, the two prime suspects for CBI Team One might have been attracted to Aarushi and possibly even fantasised about her, but the administration of the so-called truth serum might induce them to say that they *did* something, which actually never happened. There *was* no other direct evidence against any of the servants. The fingerprint on the bottle of Ballantine whiskey did not match that of Krishna, Rajkumar or indeed the Talwars. The palm print left by the killer on the terrace wall was never successfully matched with any of the crime suspects, and was allowed to be washed away by the rain.

CBI Team One may have honestly believed that the Talwars were innocent and that the associates of the servant were the ones who committed the murders but the new CBI director rightly concluded that the police could not be permitted to take the short-cut, third-degree confessional route to investigations as so often happens in India.

The Wider Implications of the Aarushi Case

It would be a shame and a waste if I confined my critique of the verdict in the Aarushi case to that particular trial and lose the opportunity to address its wider implications for similar cases of injustice in criminal trials in thousands of subordinate courts across the land.

The justice framework in this country is like a colossal glass mirror that has been smashed into smithereens. The Aarushi case represents only one of those small pieces; thousands of other small pieces lie beside it and continue to accumulate. Each small mirror carries within it a record of similar distortions in the judicial process.

A Question of Judicial Accountability

One of the more interesting quotes in Judge Shyam Lal's judgement refers to the principle of judicial accountability:

He refers to the case of *Shivaji Sahabrao Bobade and another Vs.State of Maharashtra*[120], where the Supreme Court observed: '*The judicial instrument has a public accountability. The cherished principles or golden thread of proof beyond reasonable doubt which runs through the web of our law should not be stretched morbidly to embrace every hunch, hesitancy and degree of doubt. The excessive solicitude reflected in the attitude that a thousand guilty men may go but one innocent martyr shall not suffer is a false dilemma. Only reasonable doubts belong to the accused. Otherwise any practical system of justice will break down and lose credibility with the community.*'

There is a possibility of misinterpreting the above. The point is that it is not an either/or scenario as far as the Aarushi and Hemraj murders are concerned. Yes, it can be argued, as Judge Shyam Lal apparently has, that we cannot take the logic of better-to-let-a-thousand-guilty-men-free-than-to-condemn-an-innocent-man to an extreme; on the other hand this argument cannot be possibly stretched to imply that we have to find a scapegoat to maintain public faith in the justice system *even if there is does not exist sufficient evidence* that would convince the mythical reasonable man.

In the Aarushi case in the end there was clearly no evidence beyond all reasonable doubt against either the Talwars or Hemraj's associates. It was not a case of letting someone free because of a 'niggling doubt' as has been suggested in Judge Lal's judgment.[121] That particular doubt was, to use an American idiom, as wide as a barnyard door.

This became abundantly clear when the CBI filed its closure report. If the CBI itself was unclear who was guilty, was it the place of the court to order it to file a charge sheet against the Talwars? What would have happened if the two CBI teams had not been swapped? Would the CBI have filed a charge sheet against Hemraj's friends, a case, again based entirely on circumstantial evidence?

The direction to the CBI to file a charge sheet in the Aarushi case overrode the gate-keeping function of investigative agencies. Is it for the courts to tell the police when they must prosecute even when they themselves confess that they lack sufficient evidence? It wasn't even the Sessions Court that issued this direction but a magistrate who didn't possess the judicial seniority to have herself tried the offence; perhaps this is an area where the law needs to be amended for such decisions are fraught with serious consequences. A legitimate argument can be raised that such a direction should perhaps be issued by a Sessions Court that has the power to hear the trial and pronounce a verdict. The irony here is that the CBI was a divided house and could not come to any definite conclusion internally and yet it managed to eventually convince the court!

Investigating agencies routinely prosecute cases even when 'reasonable doubt' exists; after all it is the court's business and not theirs to decide whether reasonable doubt exists in a particular case. But here, it was not that the CBI was labouring under 'reasonable doubt'; it was completely conflicted internally and it was only after careful deliberation they submitted to the court that they had no case to present at all.

Justice was subverted in the end and it became a case of – permissible in the living rooms of the chatterati perhaps but not among the legally qualified fraternity – something like take your pick, my friend, but it *has* to be one of the two choices. Someone has to be punished.

Aarushi's Relevance for Other Criminal Trials

There are two themes that affect many criminal trials across the land but happily enough they did *not* affect the Aarushi case.

The Integrity of Our Judges

The first of these relate to judicial corruption. Judge Shyam Lal's integrity cannot be questioned. He had nothing to gain personally from convicting the Talwars. Although sometimes money can change hands because someone's conviction is sought by powerful interests, say for example by a political or industrial rival to an accused person, in the vast majority of cases it is in exchange for a judicial acquittal and not a conviction. Judge Shyam Lal's post-retirement life confirms this impression of his integrity. He is a practising lawyer in the Allahabad High Court, a natural progression for a judge who doesn't wish to give up the active life. That fact alone, that Judge Lal was honest and a man of integrity does not, however, mean that his verdict was not deeply and fatally flawed, as discussed earlier.

Judge Lal's integrity is by no means representative of the state of the judiciary taken as a whole.

In an interview in 2013 former chief justice, P. Sathasivam acknowledged that the judiciary was 'not untouched by corruption'.[122] Allegations surfaced even against the sitting judge of the National Human Rights Commission (NHRC), an erstwhile Supreme Court judge[123]. Well-known and highly regarded Supreme Court lawyer Prashant Bhushan made the astounding claim that about *fifty percent* of the last sixteen or seventeen chief justices of India were involved in some or other act of corruption[124]. Be that as it may, we may fairly conclude that the apex court is not immune from the virus of corruption. As regards the subordinate judiciary, the category to which Judge Shyam Lal belongs, there is widespread corruption. The Supreme Court has often given vent to its anguish on corruption in the lower courts. In the context of a lower court decision in Delhi a division bench of Supreme Court Justices Markandey Katju and Gyan Sudha Misra observed as follows: *'A large section of subordinate judges is bringing disrepute to the entire judiciary. We have to hear of judges taking money and can do nothing but hang our heads in shame.'*[125] Another former chief justice of India, V.N. Khare spoke in an interview in 2012 on how corruption was *rampant* in the lower courts.[126] The interviewer asked him if the relevant high court wasn't responsible for allowing this to happen. He conceded that the high court inspecting judges went with a 'lot of *band baja'* but were presented with a rosy picture and often did not have time to do a proper inspection.[127]

In his courtroom Judge Shyam Lal may have been a man of integrity, but the same cannot be said about his staff. It is possible of course, but any claims that the judicial clerks emulated the judge need to be taken with a large dose of salt.

The sad truth is that judicial corruption exists in our lower courts together with en masse clerical corruption snapping at the heels of our justice system. The Aarushi case was unlikely to have been an exception.

Court clerk corruption is widespread and practically a universal phenomenon in hundreds of subordinate courts all over the country.[128] In many states across the country, money is paid to the court clerks in criminal courts for every small thing such as information on a date, having bail papers put forward, having surety approved, filing process fee for the service of summons to a defence witness, to get an application listed the next day... the list is interminable. Nothing moves without money. So much so that these small transactions are accepted as a matter of course and many court clerks have come to feel and behave as if it were their right and due. Money is given by the accused persons, the lawyer or the lawyer's clerk as a matter of routine – without a thought. It has now ceased to be thought of as a bribe.

Perjured Testimony in Criminal Trials

The other thing that did *not* happen in the Aarushi case (or to a lesser extent, if it did) is that the trial was free from perjured testimony. There were no 'stock witnesses' produced by the prosecution. Judge Lal does not deserve credit for this, since it is the task of the prosecution to produce witnesses that support its case. Should we then be congratulating the prosecution? My guess is that we should probably hold back on our compliments. In a case that was so high profile, grabbing the headlines for years on end, it would be too risky an affair to have produced the testimony of a stock witness used to deposing falsely on behalf of the police. The consequences for the image of the prosecution services would have been devastating and could have impacted the rest of the trial.

The more naïve or less knowledgeable readers may be shocked by my assertion. I could do worse than refer them to Krishna Iyer's judgement in the Paniwala case, a damning indictment of the manner in which the police and the prosecuting agencies of the state function.

The case in question, *Prem Chand Paniwala versus Union of India*[129] is of one Prem Chand, who whilst still a teenager began a small trade of selling soft drinks outside Delite Cinema on Asaf Ali Road in Delhi. According to Paniwala, as he later came to be known, in consideration for permitting him to carry on his small trade, the local police station began using him as their stock witness in numerous court cases and eventually he came to be moulded into their permanent professional witness. Paaniwala filed along with his petition hundreds of summonses, which he had received from various criminal courts in the city to appear as a witness on behalf of the state, which he had (wisely) preserved with him.[130]

Justice Krishna Iyer who heard the case became convinced that the petitioner's story had the ring of incontrovertible truth, even though he was himself a self confessed perjurer. On the factual situation Krishna Iyer observed: '*We have no doubt that the petitioner, who has given particulars of a large number of cases where he has been cited as witness is speaking the truth, even assuming that 3000 cases may be an exaggeration.*'[131] Passing severe strictures against the police department, the learned judge urged the state to issue appropriate orders to the police department to prevent such abuse of the judicial process.

The Integrity of Our Court Buildings

A few words may be said about the crumbling infrastructure of our courts and outside spaces.

In *Aarushi* Avirook Sen describes both the physical structure of the court buildings at Ghaziabad, and the general atmosphere outside, with adjacent food stalls and a gutter-emitting foul smells running close by.[132] This unsavory ambience surrounding the courts is by no means confined to Ghaziabad.

In hundreds of subordinate courts immediately outside the courts often crumbling edifice, under thatched roofs, tarpaulin or blue skies, sit the purveyors of stamp paper and the attestators of stamped documents. Keeping them company are black robed lawyers, litigants, typists and touts.

Fernando da Cruz, a colleague who works for the UN is an architect by profession. He tells me that during the years he spent working for the local government in the UK designing low-cost housing, one of the important things they kept in mind was to design buildings and spaces in such a way that it would reduce crime. At the simplest level, if you have good street lighting for example in an urban neighbourhood, you automatically reduce the risk of thefts, robberies, even acts of violence.

The fragile, run-down and overcrowded structures that currently house trial courts in most parts of our country make for an unedifying spectacle. Far from suggesting the majesty of justice, which many high court buildings do, these decrepit structures evoke the image of an institution that has been eroded and corrupted.

The Aarushi Case and the Quality of Police Investigations

In the Aarushi case the quality of investigation carried out by the UP state police was a botched up affair. The crime scene was heavily contaminated as a result of the negligence of the police. Forensic samples that could have provided direct, potentially clinching evidence were not obtained.

Was this special incompetence demonstrative just of the UP police or representative of the general state of affairs qua crime investigation in the rest of the country? Sadly enough the answer to this question is that it was probably representative and not an exception. It was only because of the high profile nature of the case that the shoddy quality of investigation came to light.

Our police force is woefully inadequate given the population and the crime rate. This is one important contributing factor to why investigations carried out by state police are often shoddy,[133] and why investigators often depend on stock witnesses to prove their cases.

There haven't been any studies that show the connection between harsh working conditions and shoddy investigations, but some reflection will suggest that such a connection can reasonably be made. After all, a man who is frustrated is less likely to derive satisfaction from work well done. He is also likely to have less regard for his fellow human beings and be more open to the use of torture while interviewing suspects.

Journalists Rhythma Kaul and Aerafa Johari wrote an important story a while ago that focused on the trials and tribulations of our police forces. It documented how across the country 'abysmal working conditions and endless work hours were pushing the khaki forces to exhaustion and despair'.[134] Studies have shown a high rate of suicide among the police. Aside from its impact on the victims, the practice of third degree torture, institutionalised and deemed 'acceptable' by our police services often leads to low self-esteem and depression resulting in suicide.

The Quality of CBI Investigations

CBI investigators are, in general, better at their job, than your average investigator in the Bihar or Uttar Pradesh police or even the Delhi police. It was for this very reason that the Aarushi murder investigation was handed over to them. There is no doubt that the caliber of the investigators and the quality of their investigation is in general several notches higher than that of the police that works under the jurisdiction of various states or Union Territories.

Part of the reason is because as understaffed as they are, they still much better staffed relative to the staffing gap that exists in most of the local state police[135]. We have very few policemen in the country relative to our needs[136]. And so when the CBI comes under stress, they too may start to perform poorly. Reports suggest that the CBI is already burdened with too many cases, as many as 9000[137]. If the CBI continues to accumulate workload without a consequent increase in qualified staff – and they are under pressure to deliver results – their performance will inevitably suffer.

Witnesses were clearly pressurised by the CBI in the Aarushi case. Torture too was deployed. This happened despite the fact that the media was watching, and high profile lawyers were representing the Talwars. Let's have a look at the allegations made with respect to the tampering of evidence in the Aarushi case.

The Things Policemen Do...

Prosecution services in India have a somewhat unique way of maintaining 'equality of arms', as the expression goes. An accused person can engage the top lawyers in the country if he can afford it. Counsel representing the state government or for that matter the CBI are often not nearly as qualified, or possessed of speaking skills useful in a trial, but no matter, they have found other ways to make up for this deficit.

Sometimes they make alterations, additions or fabrications to the record that would validate their case. Policeman Bacchu Singh practically admitted in court that he had made 'adjustments' to the signed panchnama. It wasn't an ordinary addition he made. The addition stated that Aarushi's pajama strings were untied. It was 'just to fill up the empty line,' he clarified.[138] Was that all? It may not have even occurred to Bachhu Singh that he was doing anything particularly wrong because as he confessed this is how he always did it.[139]

The second thing policemen have been known to do is compromise the exhibits to their advantage. Exhibits are supposed to be *sealed* and the seal is only supposed to be broken open in the presence of the judge when the exhibit is being brought into evidence. But of course nothing prevents the police from breaking open a seal, making the necessary 'adjustments' and then sealing things up again. In the Talwar murder case they did this with a crucial piece of evidence. The Talwars had realised that there was a forensic report which stated that the blood on the purple pillow case seized from Krishna's room had yielded Hemraj's DNA. This was a forensic development of potentially huge significance. However, the investigators had a simple response to this: It was, they maintained, quite simply a typographical error, even if it was repeated six times.[140]

The pillow cover should have remained sealed but to prove their case to the court, it was tampered. It appeared that the seal was broken and the pillow covers were resealed. This is unacceptable, but Judge Shyam Lal chose to overlook the suggestion that there may have been tampering.[141]

The police and the prosecution exhibit close cooperation, and this is how it should be. On the face of it that is fine except when it sometimes extends far beyond what is permissible under the law. In the Aarushi case, pressure was clearly brought on Mr Gautam to say things that he had not said previously. For instance in his earlier statements to the policemen he nowhere said that he had been requested to ask the doctors not to mention the word 'rape'; but in court he insisted that he had been told to do so. If there are contradictions in the statement made by a witness to the police soon after the event with the testimony of the witness in court many months or years later, these contradictions are not without significance and suggest that the testimony may not be reliable.

There is another thing at play that creates some equality of arms for prosecutors as compared with high profile and high earning defence counsel. The prosecutors and the judges are both salaried individuals. More importantly their salaries are nothing compared to the earnings of defence counsel in prestigious matters. Harish Salve, senior advocate, who appeared for the Talwars in the Supreme Court may charge as much or more for a single appearance in the apex court on behalf of a corporate client (though not for individual clients like the Talwars) than what Judge Shyam Lal and R.K. Saini, the prosecutor make in a year! The best lawyers do not chose to become judges at the lower court or session court level and would regard such an offer were it to be made with undisguised contempt (They may, however, be flattered to be considered for a position at the high court).

There is therefore inbuilt into the system some class solidarity if not mutual sympathy between the judge, the prosecutor and the investigating officer when dealing with high profile accused that are represented by high profile lawyers. Aside from this, there is of course the camaraderie that builds up due to the fact that while many different defence lawyers appear before the session courts (with the acknowledged virtuosos appearing in only the most paying and prestigious matters); the number of prosecutors on the other hand is relatively limited.

I should mention here that Bachhu Singh, the tampering policeman was eventually convicted of murder and joined Dr Rajesh Talwar in Dasna jail. Was this karmic retribution or did the law eventually catch up with this lawbreaker? Clearly tampering with evidence was a minor offence compared to some other things that he did...

Aarushi and the Shortcut Third Degree Investigation Route

Two things did not happen in the Aarushi trial that infect criminal trials not uncommonly in India. There was an absence of judicial corruption (perhaps the case was assigned to Judge Shyam Lal by the district judge keeping in mind his reputation) and there were no stock witnesses used.

One could have expected that third degree torture would also not be employed, but alas, this was not the case. It appears clear that Hemraj's associates were subjected to police brutality as an 'aid' to investigation. Their police confessions were procured through what are euphemistically referred to as 'third degree' methods. This is deeply saddening given that the media had their searchlights trained on the trial. Does this mean that we as a nation have greater tolerance for the use of torture by the police than we have for judicial corruption or perjured testimony? The torture of Krishna and Rajkumar took place under the very nose of the media (just as sometimes judicial clerks accept bribes under the very nose of the judge). Was this use of torture in the Aarushi case an exceptional measure resorted to only in the Aarushi case? By no means.

Towards the end of 2013 the Supreme Court became extremely concerned with the ineffective implementation of a series of directions to curb custodial deaths. The shocking news that nearly 12,000 persons died – either in jail or police stations – in the last five years galvanised the court to seek an urgent explanation from the Center and the States.[142]

The majority of the 12,000 cases of persons who died in police custody would have been victims of police torture. Torture cases over the same period that did not result in death could reasonably be expected to be in the hundreds of thousands.

Data suggests that in police stations all over the country, prisoners are commonly administered what has come to be known as third degree methods by the police almost as a matter of routine. Third degree, which is nothing but torture plain and simple has infinite possibilities, depending upon the cruelty and ingenuity of its perpetrators. Thus it is not uncommon to read horrendous accounts of prisoners being hung upside down and having sticks shoved up private parts or being subjected to electric shock treatment.

Third degree is torture, which no human being, criminal or otherwise ought to be subjected to. Not only can there therefore be no legal sanction for such inhuman practices in any civilised nation's jurisprudence, the police force itself commits a serious crime when it takes recourse to such brutalised behaviour as an aid in the detection, prevention and investigation of crime. In fact, generally speaking, inflicting third degree torture is a far more serious crime than the crime sought to be investigated. The crime of corruption pales before it.

Aarushi, and the Delays in our Rotting Justice Delivery System

When will the Talwars' appeal to the Allahabad High Court come up for hearing? Estimates range from ten to thirty years, given the backlog.[143] It is true that there are other high courts that perform better but even their backlog is not up to acceptable standards. Neither is the Allahabad High Court alone; Rajasthan High Court takes an equivalent number of years in disposing off appeals.

News travels fast, and so do reputations in the age of the Internet. India's poor reputation for justice delivery is now well known throughout the world and undermines our status as a would-be super power. A Britisher who was left paralysed in the 26/11 attacks in Mumbai won the right to have his case for damages heard in the UK on the basis that the Indian justice system was dysfunctional. It is not an occasion for Indian lawmakers and intellectuals to react with anger and misguided patriotism at this verdict but rather to acknowledge the terrible truth about our courts. He fell fifty feet from the window of his room in the Taj in a bid to escape the terrorists.[144] He filed a claim against the Tata Group that owns the Taj Mahal Hotel in Mumbai. The high court in England accepted his plea and argument that taking his case through the Indian courts ***could take upto 20 years.***[145]

This is how the world assesses India; and it does not have any vested interest here in projecting India in an unfavourable light. If anyone has issue with the second half of the title to this book 'The Murder of Justice' I would ask him to merely consider this:

A sentence of life imprisonment has no meaning in India in the context of our system of appeals. If you are convicted and sentenced to prison (and do not get bail) *you anyhow receive a life sentence*, for that is how long it will take for your appeal to come up for hearing before the high court (leave aside the Supreme Court for the time being).

There are those who point out (accurately) that we have too many appeals in this country. People rush off to the Supreme Court and file a Special Leave Petition (SLP) – the Talwars too did this – for each and every small issue. However consider this. For those who receive a sentence of life imprisonment (unless they are at some stage granted bail) the trial court verdict is more or less final because their life term will be close to expiring by the time their appeal is heard. *It doesn't even matter that an appellate procedure exists.*

Aarushi: What is Being Done to Reduce Delays in Criminal Trials?

Has the government learnt any lesson from the Aarushi case in terms of reducing delays in the courts? The question is largely rhetorical and it goes without saying that it hasn't. Cases continue to drag on endlessly and it is not even that there is no solution. Everyone knows the solution and they are regularly discussed for there is no political will to do it.

A gathering takes place in Delhi every couple of years with lunches and dinners thrown in, where justices from the Supreme Court and high courts dine and deliberate on the need for judicial reform. Food for thought and action one would imagine, but this has been happening for as long as I can remember. The central issue remains the same – delay at the courts. But does anything concretely and substantial happen on the ground as a consequence? The answer is sadly enough, an emphatic no.

In 1985, an Extraordinary Conference of Chief Justices of the various high courts and chief ministers and law ministers was held to consider what could be done about a backlog of more than ten million cases. In 2013 too, the papers reported on how on 7 April 'at least 24 Chief Justices of High Courts and 28 judges from the Supreme Court deliberated for two days on the urgent need to ensure a more efficient justice delivery system'.[146] More conferences with dinners will discuss these issues this year and in the years ahead.

Now and again the Supreme Court raps the lower judiciary for delays. A report speaks of how 'at a time when people are getting impatient with judicial delays, the Supreme Court has stepped in to curb the tendency of trail courts to liberally grant adjournments at the instance of lawyers'.[147]

Is this a case of the pot calling the kettle black? Supreme Court lawyer and jurist of repute Dr Rajeev Dhawan points out in the context of the Supreme Court how 'one of its biggest problems has been the challenge of arrears before it.'[148] After all even in the Sanjay Dutt case, of the twenty years that the case took before a final verdict ten years later, *roughly half that time was spent in the Supreme Court.* Why so long? It was waiting its turn in the queue. Why does the Supreme Court never apologise for the delays caused by the apex court itself?

Dealing with arrears in the Supreme Court and high courts is essential but even more essential is reducing the average length of criminal trials and civil cases in the trial courts. After all, these are the courts that matter the most in a sense since they concern the average citizen, your common man. Relative to the hundreds of thousands of cases pending in the lower courts only a very small percentage of these manage to find their way up the appeal ladder all the way up to the Supreme Court.

Even the government's own figures are dismaying. Look at these figures, for instance, quoted in a news report.[149] The number of cases pending in trial courts has crossed 2.68 crores. There are almost four thousand judicial vacancies. The average time taken in criminal cases is between five-eight years at the trial court level and then there seems to be a never-ending queue of appeals at the level of the high court and the Supreme Court. In the case of high profile crimes sometimes fast track courts are appointed. There is, however, a need to fast track ALL criminal cases.

Now the question arises: Is it really possible to fast track all cases?

Yes, it is.

A plan by the chief justice to double the number of judges over the next five years will fall woefully short of requirements. We don't have such a resource crunch as say Ethiopia but our judge-population ration is very similar. If we need to have a six-lane highway anticipating that there will be more cars in the years to come, we also need to have more judges from the outset and not try and quick fix the situation at a later stage where the situation has once again become critical. The other thing worth mentioning here is that in India we quite often fall short of target. If we aim for a six fold increase it will not surprise anyone if we attain only a five fold increase or even four times. To adapt an American saying, if you aim for the sky you will at least hit the roof!

The United States has a judge-population ratio that is *ten* times higher than our own. Our population will continue to rise at a faster rate and more importantly as our legal system starts to deliver justice, there will be a spiraling effect. As the US jurist Marc Galanter who has studied the issue extensively points out contrary to popular belief India has one of the lowest filing rates in the world.[150]

Investment will be needed not only to pay the salaries to six times the number of judges as exist at the present moment, there will need to be a corresponding investment in the clerical and support staff servicing the judiciary. Courtrooms will be needed to house additional judges.

This means new buildings, more computers, furniture, law libraries and so on and forth. Right now the infrastructure at the trial courts across the country is crumbling. Everything is in a shambles. Lawyers sit outside under the open sky without proper offices together with court typists, notary publics, oath commissioners. Something needs to be done for these court functionaries.

Six times the existing number of judges and the corresponding investment in court buildings, infrastructure, support staff, will barely prove enough, for we also need to greatly improve what already exists! The expansion of the judiciary cannot take place at once, but it must take place, quite literally, on a war footing.

If we need more judges there is also a crying need for more prosecutors and more investigators. We need thousands of additional policemen. The judge-population ratio and the police-population ratio in India are both abysmally low.

Why Are The Solutions Not Being Implemented?

Since everyone knows that part of the solution towards solving the backlog of criminal cases is increasing the number of judges and policemen and housing them in better buildings, why is this not being done? There is no political will, but that begs a further question – why is there no political will.

The short answer to this question is that our state assemblies across the land are full of representatives with a criminal record. There are many of our political representatives in the Lok Sabha and Rajya Sabha who also have criminal cases pending against them. Many employ an army of hoodlums during election time who also have criminal cases pending against them. An efficient system of justice means that all these people will be convicted, or at least will have the possibility of a speedy conviction hanging over them. Not to spend too much time discussing why these legal reforms are not being implemented, since it is outside the scope of the present book, one can sum up the reasons in a few words; they will benefit the people but not their political representatives.

DNA Testing in India Needs to be Developed

The sad truth is that although DNA sampling has now become very sophisticated it was not used properly in the Aarushi case. According to a guide issued by the American National Forensic Science Technology Center, with the advancement of technology, it is now possible for forensic scientists to analyse smaller and smaller biological samples and develop a DNA profile[151]. Take an example. If a person touched an object or weapon skin cells may have been left behind. Sometimes this low level DNA is referred to as 'touch DNA'. It was therefore not only the bloodied fingerprint on the terrace wall, the finger prints on the cooler panel or on the lock to the terrace door, the crime scene both at the terrace and the Talwars' apartment was simply awash with low level DNA. As an emerging superpower India needs to hone up its DNA testing skills. There were fingerprints found on the Ballantine whiskey bottle that could not be matched with any of the suspects including the Talwars (CBI Closure Report). Was an attempt made to see if the same unidentified fingerprint was found elsewhere, in Aarushi's bedroom or on the terrace? Unfortunately, my question is rhetorical. No attempt was even made. Had this unidentified fingerprint been found all over the place, it could have given credence to the outsider theory. As yet we do not even have a developed DNA database. In cases where the DNA does not match any suspect, in the US that DNA profile is entered into the FBI's combined DNA Index system. Nothing similar exists here. A start needs to be made by the creation of a Forensic Science Oversight Commission to make sure that state forensic laboratories are properly insulated from pressure from prosecutorial and investigative agencies. A Forensic Science Ethical Code also needs to be established.

It is worthwhile mentioning that there is a relationship here between DNA testing and torture. As DNA profiling technology develops, it will hopefully reduce the need for torture and stock witnesses so often resorted to by the police.

Technology should also be used to track down cases where inordinate delays are taking place. It is well known amongst lawyers that any litigant who has a bad case tries to drag it out for as long as possible. There are all kinds of delaying tactics that are employed by lawyers, but oftentimes judges too don't monitor cases properly.

The Need to Convict Someone, Anyone

Analysing the entire Aarushi affair, in the end it could be said that there was a need to convict someone, *anyone*, to sustain the public's faith in the judiciary. The government could simply not afford to have a situation where finally at the end of the day no one was convicted. It was part of the reason why such a high-ranking officer, a person with the rank of deputy inspector general was put in charge of investigations the first time around. DIG Arun Kumar was someone who had investigated the famous Telgi scam a case of forged stamp papers which ran into billions of rupees; a mere homicide even if covered extensively in the national media was beneath him! Yet the stakes were high for the credibility of the government. Not being able to find and convict the killers would erode confidence in the justice system, in the police – and by extension of the same logic the government itself.

It could be said that this need to pin the blame on someone, to find a scapegoat, as the expression goes is inversely proportional to how well the justice system in a country actually functions. If we actually had a justice system in India that worked well, an occasional police malfunction and failure to convict someone in the case of a heinous crime, could be absorbed and accepted by the ordinary man on the street, and he could still retain faith in the system. But our justice system is anyhow so flawed and dysfunctional that the powers-that-be cannot afford for its failings to be exposed yet further.

The CBI demonstrated institutional courage in submitting a closure report that in all fairness they could not make out a case against anyone. Ghaziabad Magistrate Preeti Singh may have sensed the public pressure (if not experienced it directly from the men in political office). Her decision to not accept the closure report was, however, one made in her own wisdom.

This idea that someone, anyone, needs to be convicted is dangerous, and fatally flawed. Had the Talwars, Krishna and Rajkumar all been let off and it was publicly declared that the Aarushi case is unsolved the government would have been under enormous pressure to take action to remedy the functioning of the police and the courts. With the conviction of the Talwars, pretence can be maintained that our justice delivery system works well – and business can carry on as usual.

Perhaps the Talwars will have justice one day, but it will not happen in this world, and no one can testify as to what happens in the after world, or if it even exists. In this world even if the high court accepts their appeal and grants them an acquittal, it will be a case of too little and far too late. Nothing can bring back to them their lost years of freedom, nothing can heal the suffering, the ignominy and agony to which they have been subjected, and finally perhaps nothing can ever compensate for the loss of their beloved daughter under the most tragic and brutal of circumstances.

Notes

1. 'No house, no family, paraded like a zoo animal in front of VIPs,' *Deccan Chronicle,* 8 July, 2015.
2. Avirook Sen, 'Aarushi,' Penguin Books Pvt Ltd, 2015; at page 293.
3. 'Supreme Court censures V K Singh,' The Hindu, 24 October, 2013.
4. Justice Katju, 'It's time to amend law on contempt of court,' *The Times of India,* 28 July, 2014.
5. As quoted in the above blog.
6. R. Vs Commissioner of Police (1968) 2QB 150.
7. Chandra Mohan Upadhaya, 'Human Rights in Pre-trial Detention,' Ashish Publishing House, 1999, at page 70.
8. Ibid.
9. Ibid.
10. 'According to CBI theory, this is how Dr Rajesh Talwar killed Aarushi and Hemraj,'*India Today,* May issue, 2008.
11. Elisabeth Kubler-Ross and David Kessler, 'On Grief and Grieving: Finding the Meaning of Grief through the Five Stages of Loss,' Scribner, 2014; page 10.
12. 'From Talwars calls nothing seemed amiss,' *The Times of India,* 27 May, 2008.
13. 'Did Aarushi shoot her killer that night,' *Mumbai Mirror,* 17 June, 2008.
14. Patrick French, 'Worse than a Daughters Death,'*Open the Magazine,* 5 February, 201.
15. Page 168 of Judge Shyam Lal's judgment.
16. Avirook Sen, 'Aarushi,' Penguin Books Pvt Ltd, 2015 page 26.
17. Ibid: page 274.
18. Ibid; page 171.
19. Ibid; page 178.
20. Ibid.
21. Ibid: page 66.
22. Ibid.
23. Ibid; pages 208-209.
24. Kathy McCoy and Charles Wibbelsman, 'The Teenage Body Book,' Hatherleigh Press, 2008; at page 23.
25. Judge Shyam Lal's judgment; page 103.
26. Avirook Sen, 'Aarushi,' Penguin Books Pvt Ltd; at page 89.

27. Judge Shyam Lal's judgment; page 54.
28. Ibid.
29. 'Aarushi murder: what the CBI found and what it could not,' MSN India, 11 February, 2011.
30. Ibid.
31. Judgment in Aarushi case; page 9.
32. Ibid; page 112.
33. Ibid; page 113.
34. Avirook Sen, 'Aarushi,' Penguin Books Pvt Ltd; at page 117.
35. Judge Shyam Lal's judgment; page 120.
36. Ibid; page 88.
37. Ibid: page 141.
38. Ibid: pages 139-142.
39. Judgment in Aarushi case; page 8.
40. Pallavi Polanki, 'Why wasn't LCN testing used in Aarushi-Hemraj investigation?' *First Post,* 20 January, 2012.
41. Avirook Sen, 'Aarushi,' *Penguin Books Pvt Ltd*, 2015 page 165.
42. Ibid: page 141.
43. 'Horror as man uses missing wife's cell to locate her car,' *Daily Mail.*, 10 August, 2012.
44. Rishika Baruah, 'First on Record, CBI's Arun Kumar, We had no proof against Talwars,' *The Quint,* 16 May, 2016.
45. Section 169 of the Criminal Procedure Code.
46. Avirook Sen, 'Aarushi,' *Penguin Books Pvt Ltd*, 2015 page 221.
47. Judgment in Aarushi case; page 16.
48. Ibid; page 104.
49. Ibid; page 14.
50. Ibid: page 19.
51. Ibid; page 32.
52. (1978) SCR (3) 207.
53. Ibid.
54. Ibid; page 101.
55. Ibid.
56. 2013 (80) ACC 138 (SC).
57. Avirook Sen, 'Aarushi,' *Penguin Books Pvt Ltd*, 2015; pages 64-65.
58. (1974) 4 SCC 267; also cited by Judge Shyam Lal.
59. Wharton's Criminal Evidence (Vol. 1 of the 12th Edn.); page 31.
60. Judgment in Aarushi case: page 63.
61. Ibid: page 78.
62. AIR 1938 All. 252.
63. Judgment in Aarushi case: page 147.

64. Avirook Sen, 'Aarushi,' *Penguin Books Pvt Ltd*, 2015; page 154.
65. Ibid.
66. Ibid.
67. Ibid.
68. Ibid; at page 151.
69. Judgment in Aarushi case; at page 101.
70. Ibid.
71. Avirook Sen, 'Aarushi,' *Penguin Books Pvt Ltd*, 2015; page 154.
72. 'Aarushi trial: Others apart from Talwars, Hemraj were present, says defence,' *Firstpost*, 8 November, 2013.
73. Avirook Sen, 'Aarushi,' *Penguin Books Pvt Ltd*, 2015; page 151.
74. Judgment in Aarushi case; page 91.
75. Ibid; at page 93.
76. *State of MP versus Ramesh and another*, (2011) 5 SCR 1.
77. Avirook Sen, 'Aarushi,' *Penguin Books Pvt Ltd*, 2015; page 151.
78. Sayantan Chakravarty, 'Stamp of Deceit,'*India Today,* 10 March, 2003.
79. Sunetra Choudhury, 'Aarushi case: Investigator breaks silence, syas he believes parents innocent,' NDTV, October 6, 2015.
80. Note: The sequence of events narrated here is partially based on how it has been presented in the film Talvar. There are some additions made to make it more credible.
81. Judgment in Aarushi case; page 170.
82. Ibid: page 14.
83. Damayanti Dutta, 'Aarushi-Hemraj case,'*India Today,*30 November, 2013.
84. 'Second polygraph test on Nupur Talwar,' *The Hindu,* 26 June, 2008.
85. 'Test after test, no results,' *The Hindustan Times,* 25 June, 2008.
86. Avirook Sen, 'Aarushi,' *Penguin Books Pvt Ltd*, 2015; at page 28.
87. 'Read for Yourself: CBI''s Aarushi's Closure Report,' News 18, 10 February, 2011.
88. Avirook Sen, 'Aarushi,' *Penguin Books Pvt Ltd*, 2015; at page 28.
89. Ibid; page 29.
90. Ibid; page 54.
91. Ibid; page 31.
92. Ibid; page 221.
93. Ibid: page 30.
94. Paul Peachey, 'Privatisation of forensic services threat to justice,' *The Independent*, 21 January, 2015.
95. 'Improving the practice and use of forensic science,' *The Justice Project*, 2015.
96. Ibid.
97. Connie Schultz, 'Another slap in the face of Justice,'PLAIN DEALER, 2 September, 2004.

98. 'CBI got edited footage of Krishna Narco-test' *The Asian Age,* 26 October, 2015
99. Ibid.
100. Ibid.
101. 'Ex CBI officer asked me to confess to murders,' *The Hindustan Times,* 24 October, 2015.
102. Sectinss 24, 25 and 26 of the Indian Evidence Act deal with how confessions to a police officer or caused by inducement threat or promise are not admissible in law.
103. https://www.cia.gov/library/center-for-the-study-of-intelligence/kent-csi/vol5no2/html/v05i2a09p_0001.htm.
104. Ibid.
105. 2010 (7) SCC 263).
106. Ibid.
107. *Selvi versus State of Karnataka*; para 16..
108. 204 Report of the Working Party of the British Psychological Society (BPS); at page 10.
109. *Selvi versus State of Karnataka*; para 47.
110. Ibid: para 46.
111. Ibid; para 223.
112. 2013 (80) ACC 138 (SC).
113. CBI Closure Report; also see Avirook Sen, 'Aarushi,' page 34.
114. Ibid.
115. Avirook Sen, 'Aarushi,' at page 90.
116. Akash Vashist, 'My hubby saw Aarushi as his own daughter: Hemraj's wife,' *India Today,* 28 March, 2011.
117. 'CBI to grill former domestic help for leads,' *Mail Today*, 2 June, 2010.
118. Ibid.
119. 'Maid murder: Trial for ex-MP, wife starts 2 July, *The Times of India,* 7 June, 2015.
120. (1973) 2 SC 793.
121. Judgment in Aarushi case; page 154.
122. J. Venktesan, 'Judiciary not untouched by corruption,' *The Hindu,* July 1, 2013.
123. 'Notice to Centre to sack Balakrishnan as NHRC chief,' *The Hindu,* 27 August 2013.
124. J. Venkatesaan, 'Not contempt of court, says Prashant Bhushan,' *The Hindu,* 19 September, 2010.
125. Gyanant Singh, 'Supreme Court wants corrupt judges thrown out,' *Mail Today,* 11 May, 2011.
126. Chandrani Bannerjee, 'Corruption is rampant in the lower courts,' *Outlook Magazine,* 1 July 2009.
127. Ibid.
128. '80 percent of lower judiciary is corrupt,' *The Telegraph,* 11 July, 2011.

129. AIR 1981 SC 613.
130. Ibid.
131. Ibid; pg 619.
132. Avirook Sen, 'Aarushi,' Penguin Books Pvt Ltd; at page 154.
133. AIR 1981 SC 619.
134. Rhythma Kaul and Aarefa Johari, 'A National Cop-out,' *The Sunday Hindustan Times,* 8 December, 2013.
135. Devesh K Pandey, 'CBI seeks greater autonomy, more skilled hands,' *The Hindu,* 14 June, 2014.
136. Rhythma Kaul and Aarefa Johari, 'A National Cop-out,' *The Sunday Hindustan Times,* 8 December, 2013.
137. 'Supreme Court restores 9000 trials in CBI Courts, *The Hindu,* 11 November, 2013.
138. Avirook Sen, 'Aarushi,' Penguin Books Pvt Ltd; at page 126.
139. Ibid.
140. Ibid: at page 194.
141. Ibid: at page 197.
142. Dhananjay Mahapatra, '11,820 custodial deaths in five years, *The Times of India*, 24 November, 2013.
143. 'Delay in hearing appeals as good as justice denied,' *The Times of India,* 15 October, 2015.
144. Prasun Sonwalkar, '26/11 victim wins right to sue Taj in UK court,' Hindustan Times, 20 December, 2013.
145. Ibid.
146. *TNN,* April 7, 2013.
147. 'Curb adjournments, speed up trials, SC tells trial courts,' *The Times of India,* 15 May, 2013.
148. Dr Rajeev Dhawan, 'A Workload Fix for the Supreme Court,' *India Today,* March 11, 2013.
149. Dhananjay Mahapatra, 'Courb Adjournments, Speed up Justice, SC tells lower courts,' *The Times of India*, 14 May 2013.
150. Krishnan Jayant K, and Galanter Marc, 'Bread for the Poor: Access to Justice and the Rights of the Needy in India,' *Indiana University, Maurier School of Law Faculty Publications,* (2004) Paper 380.
151. 'A Simplified Guide to DNA Evidence,' Issued by National Forensic Science Technology Center, USA.